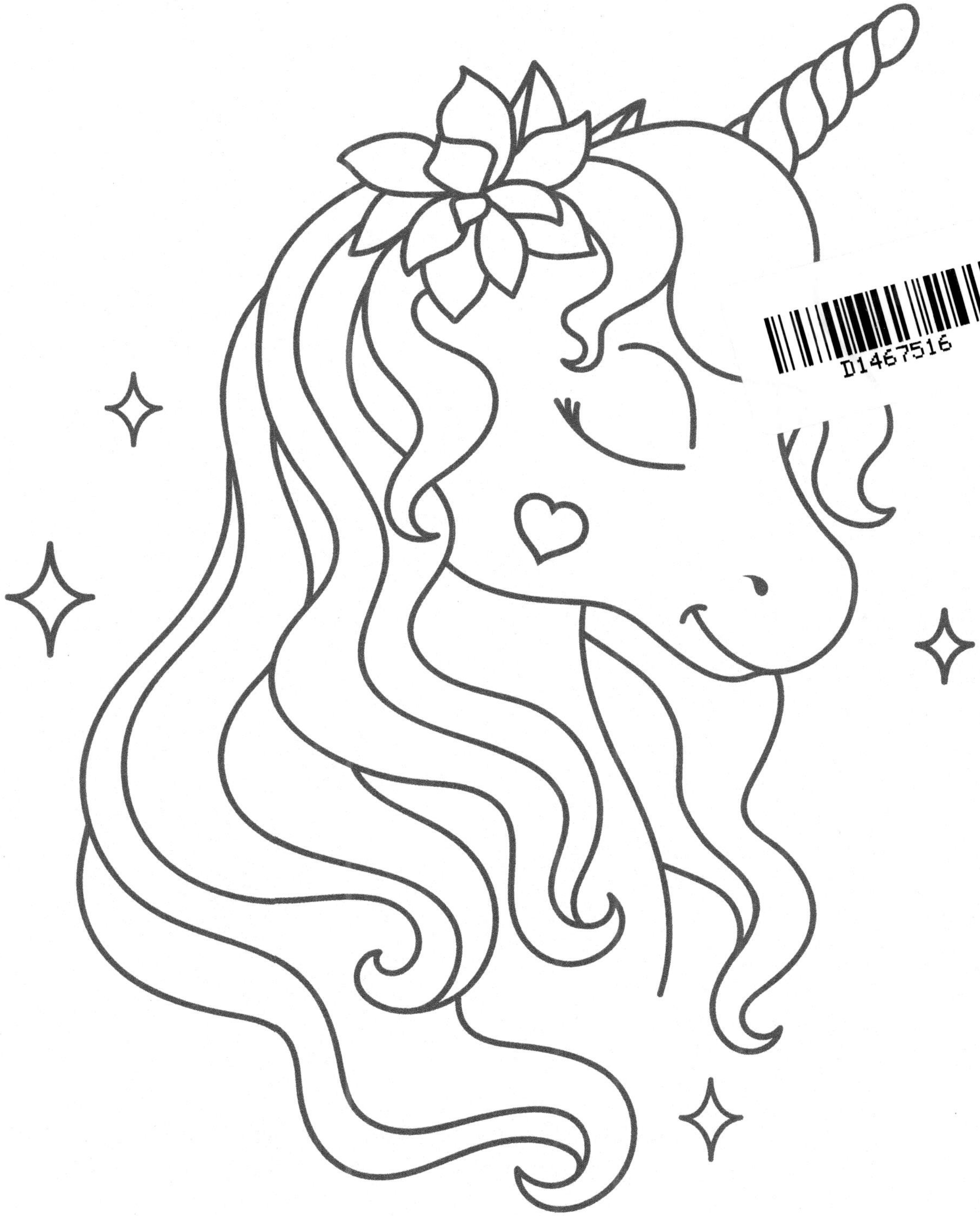

BIG SISTER!

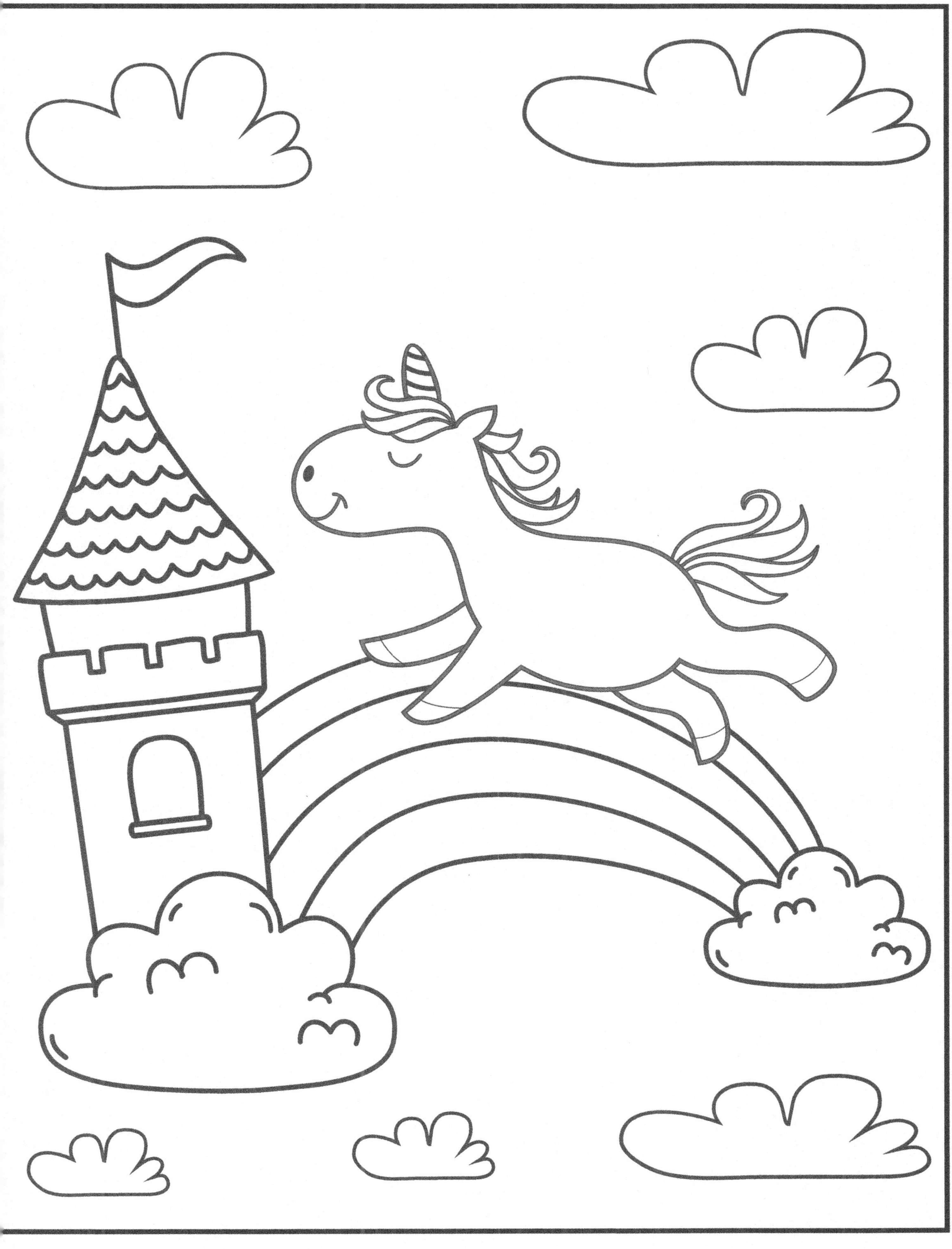

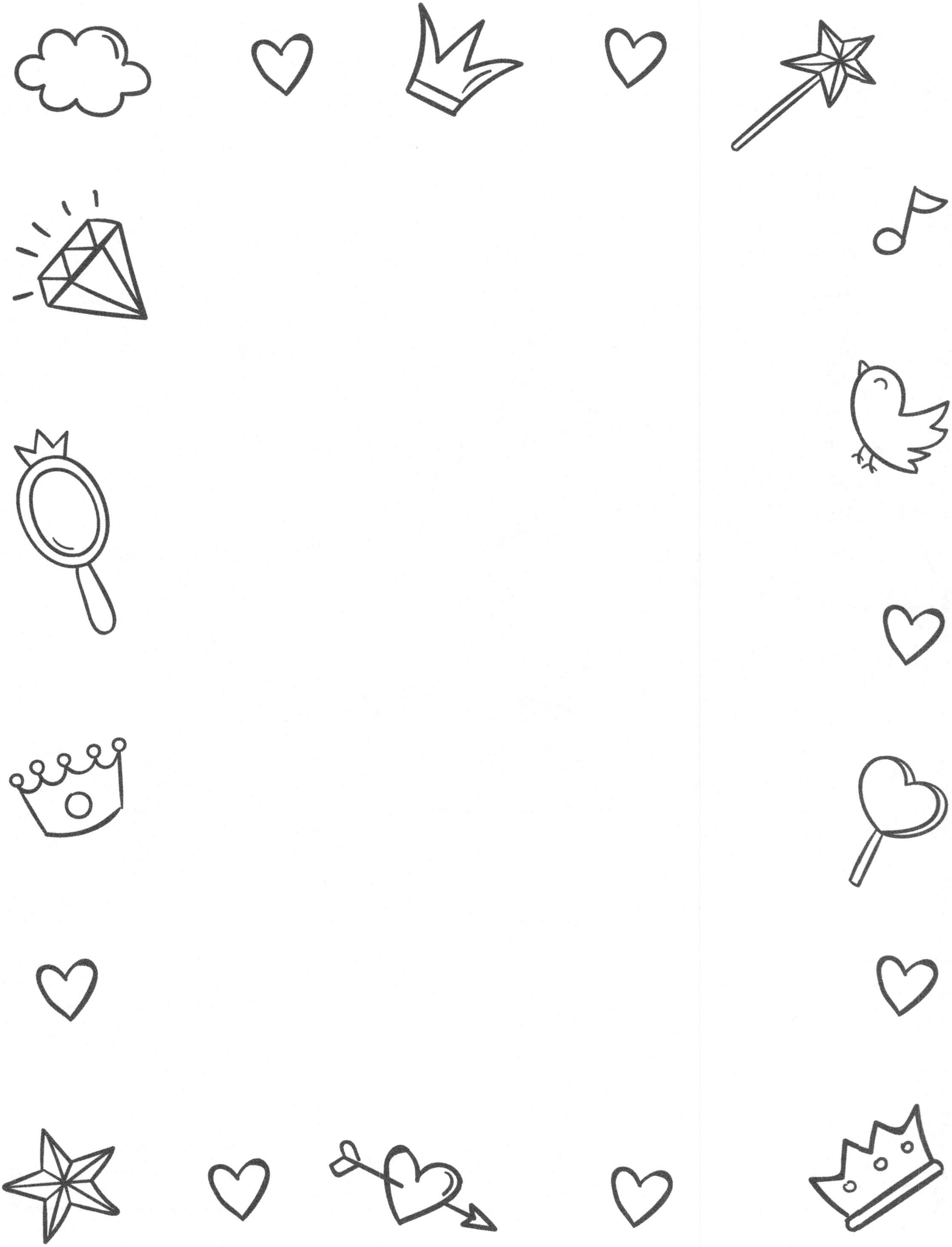

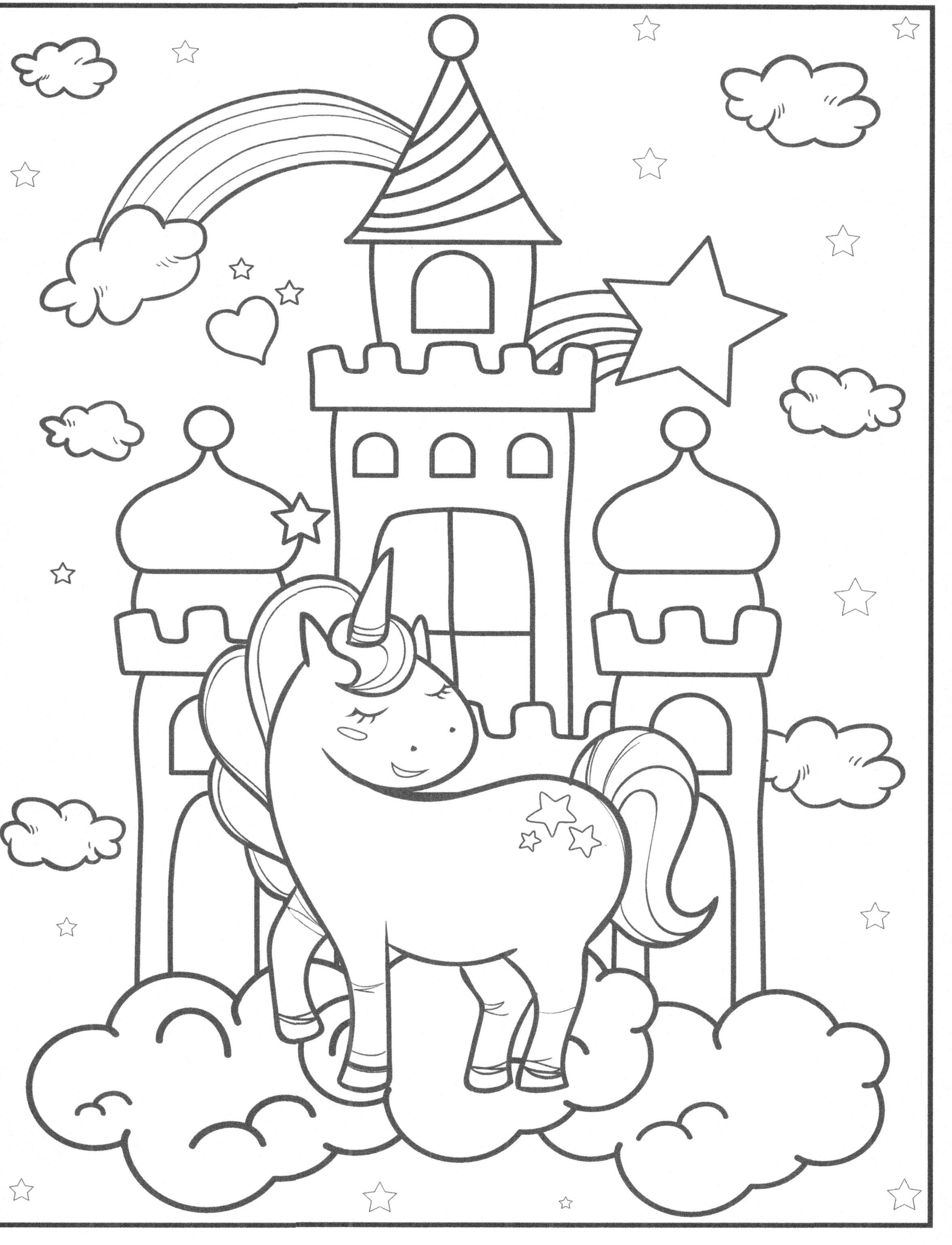

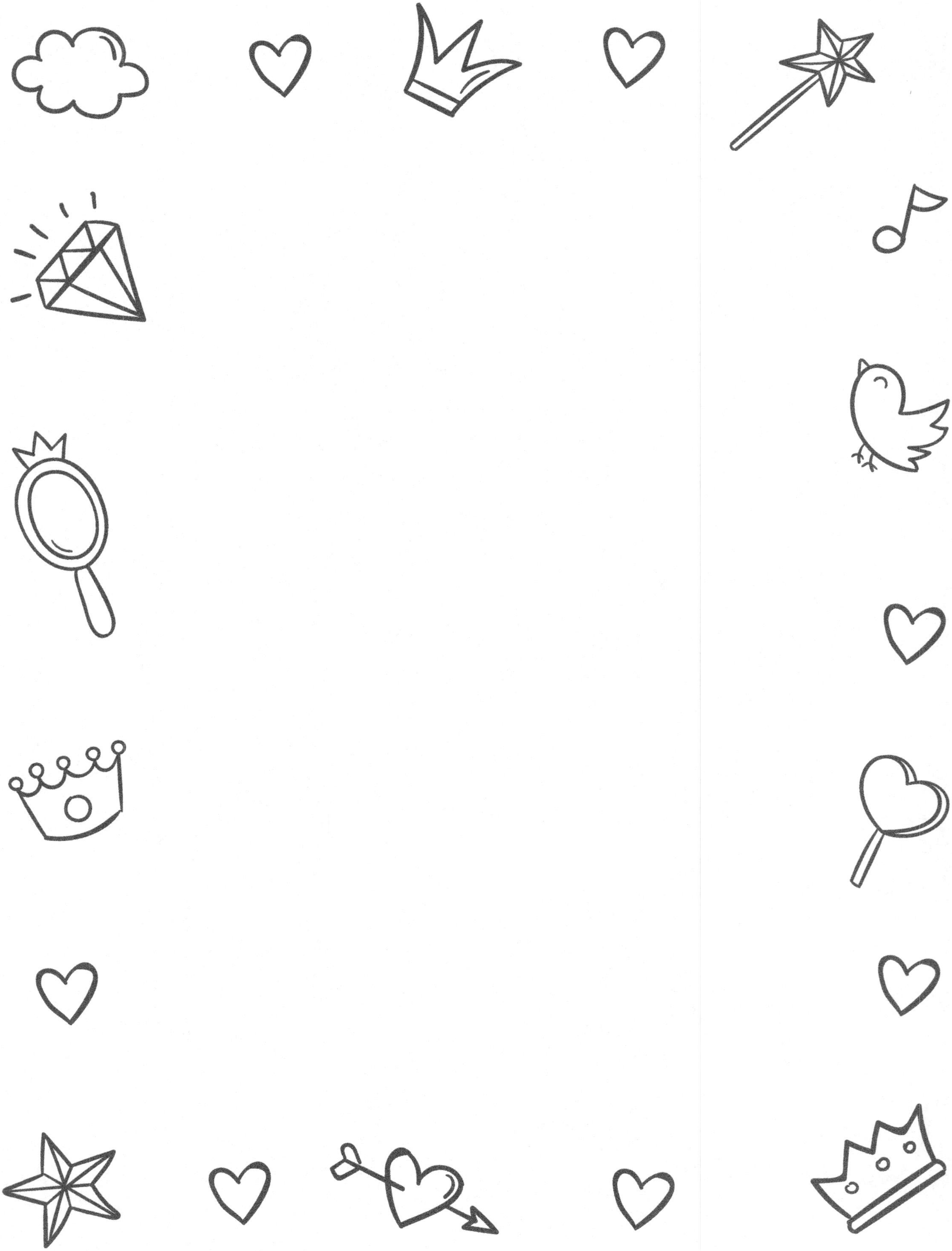

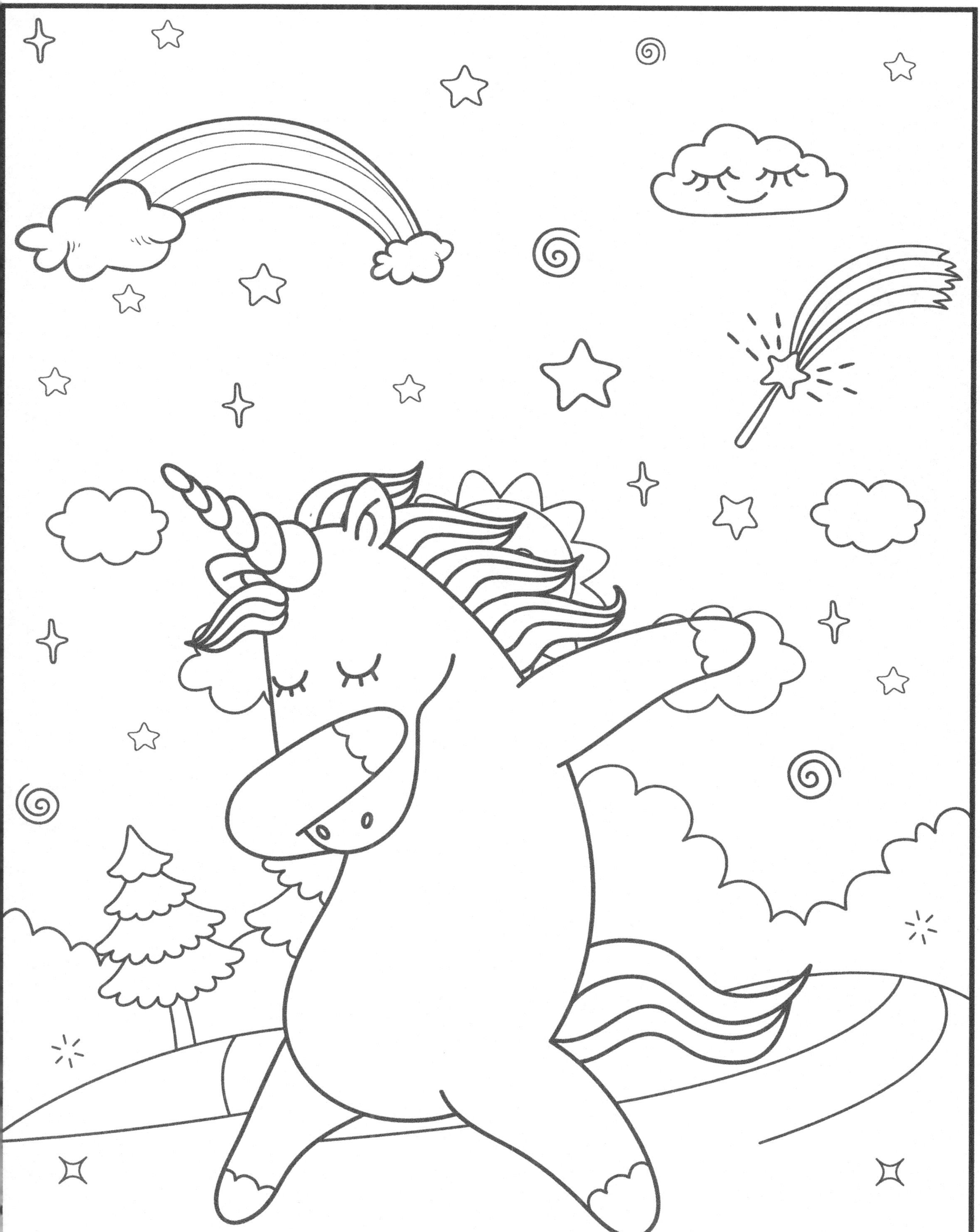

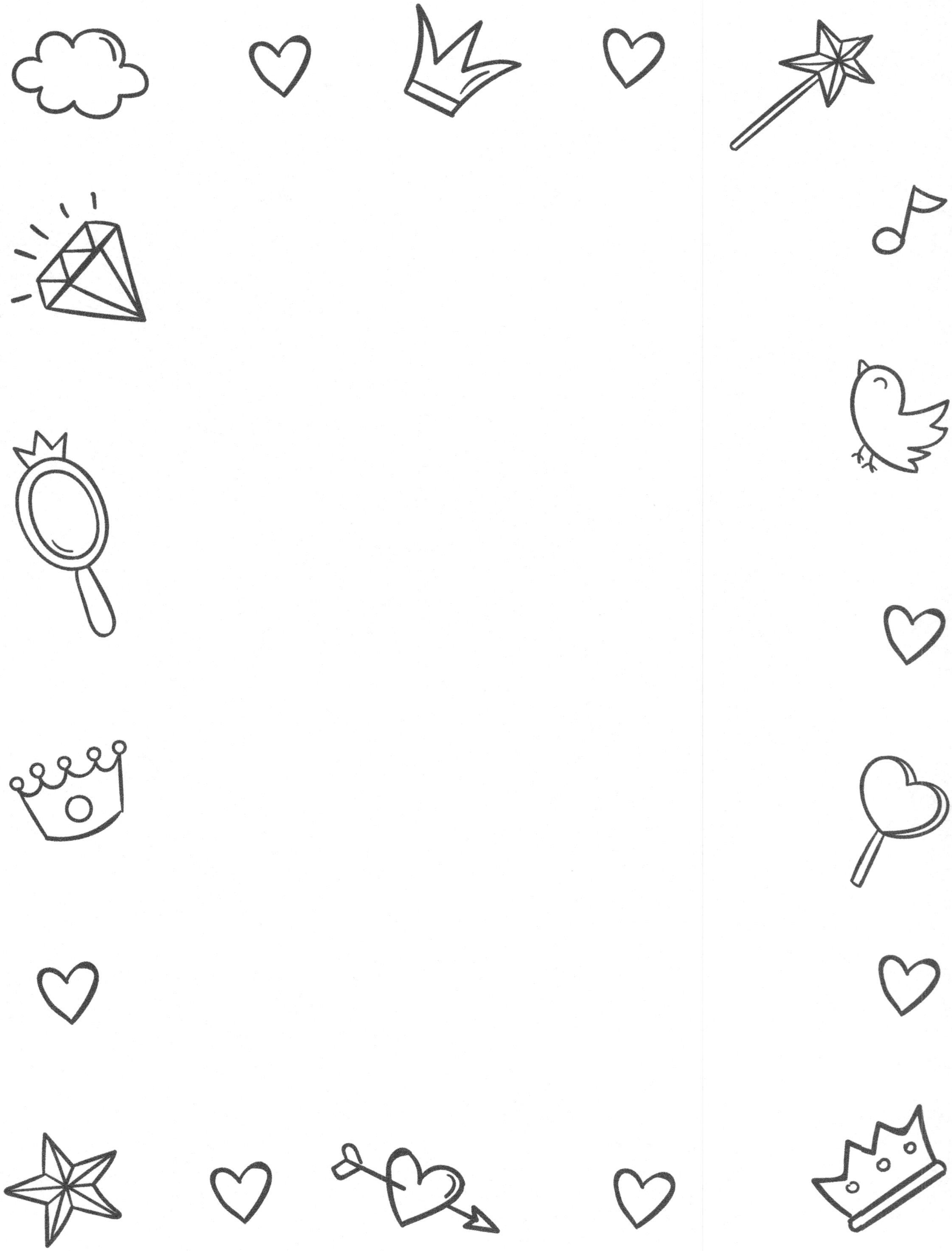

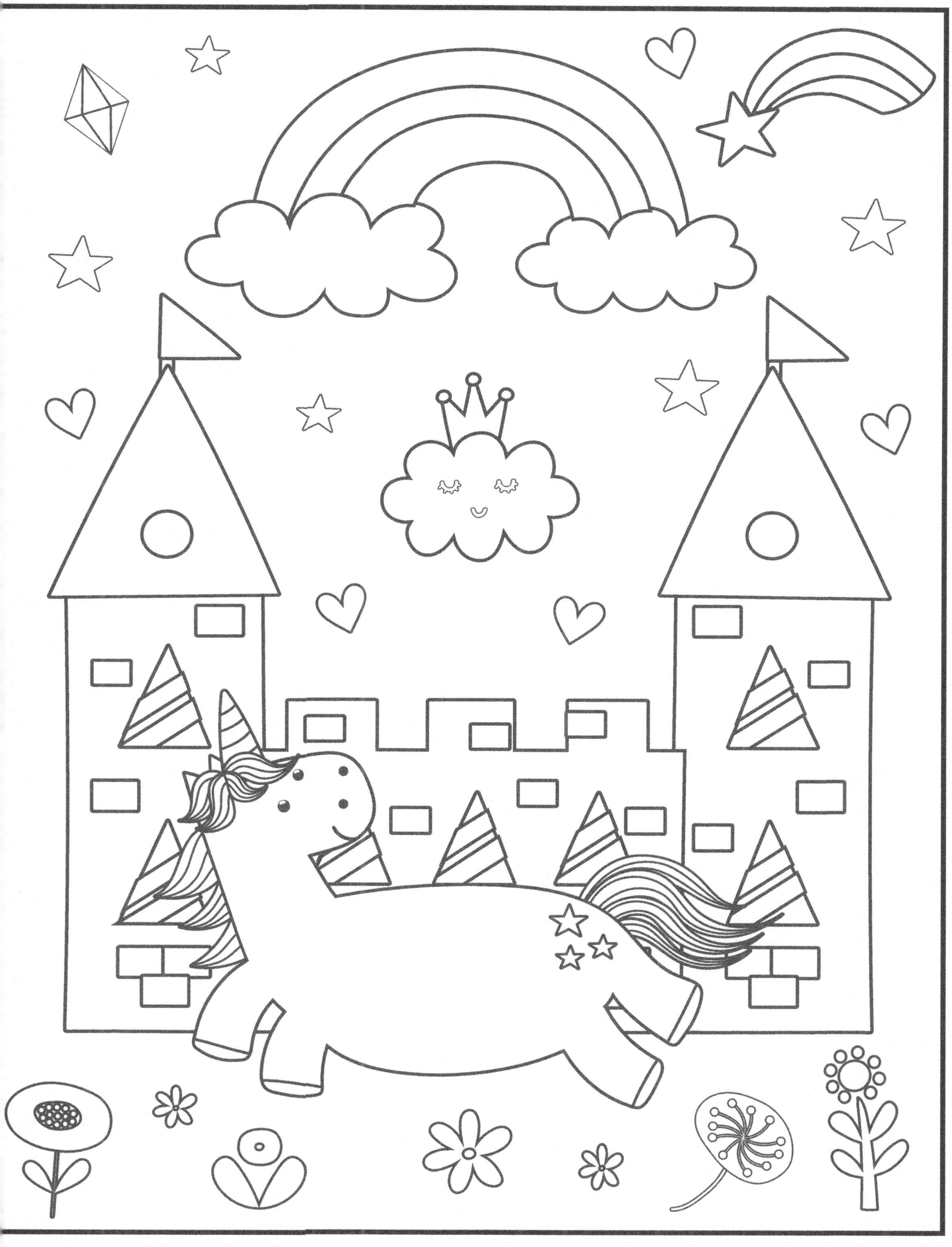

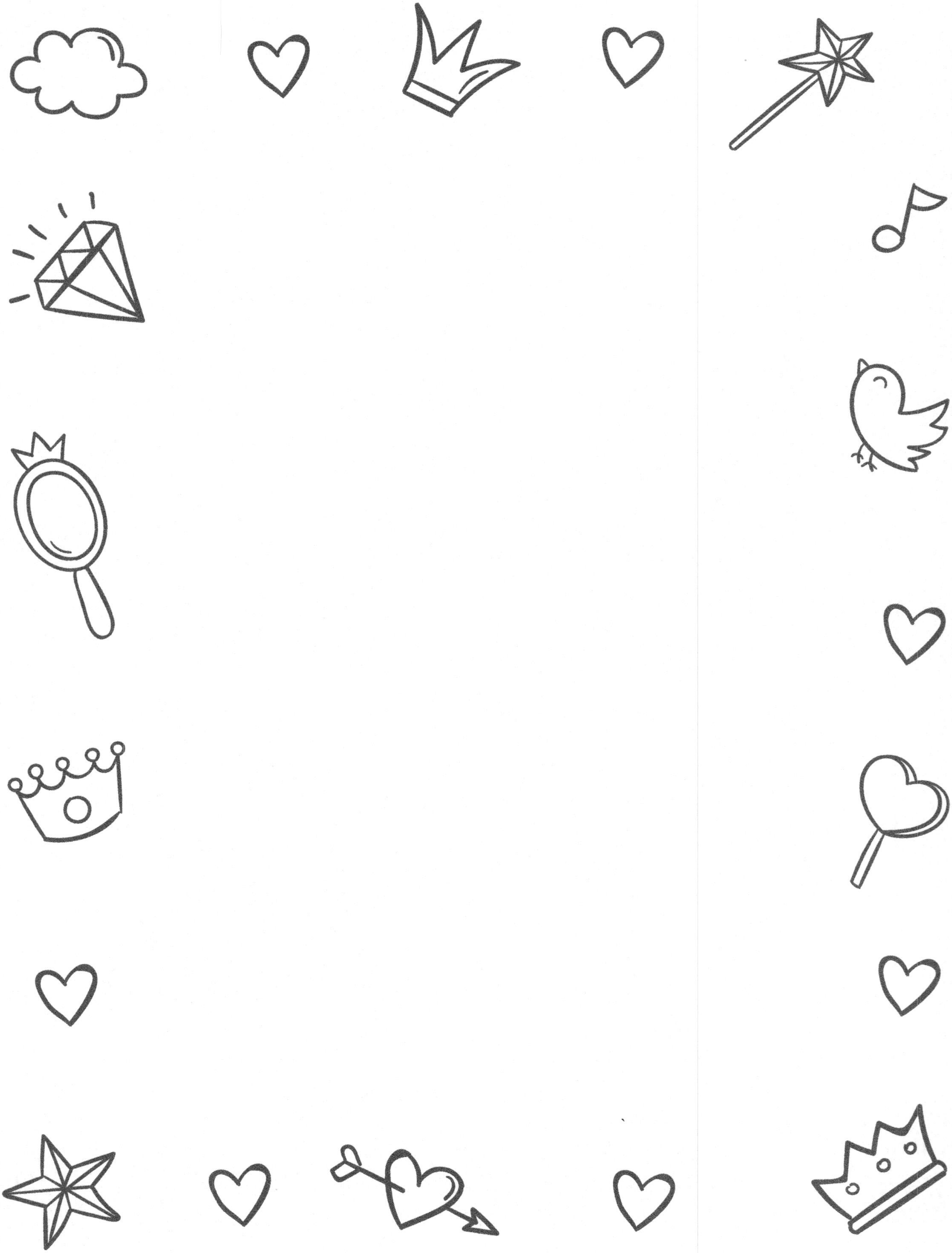

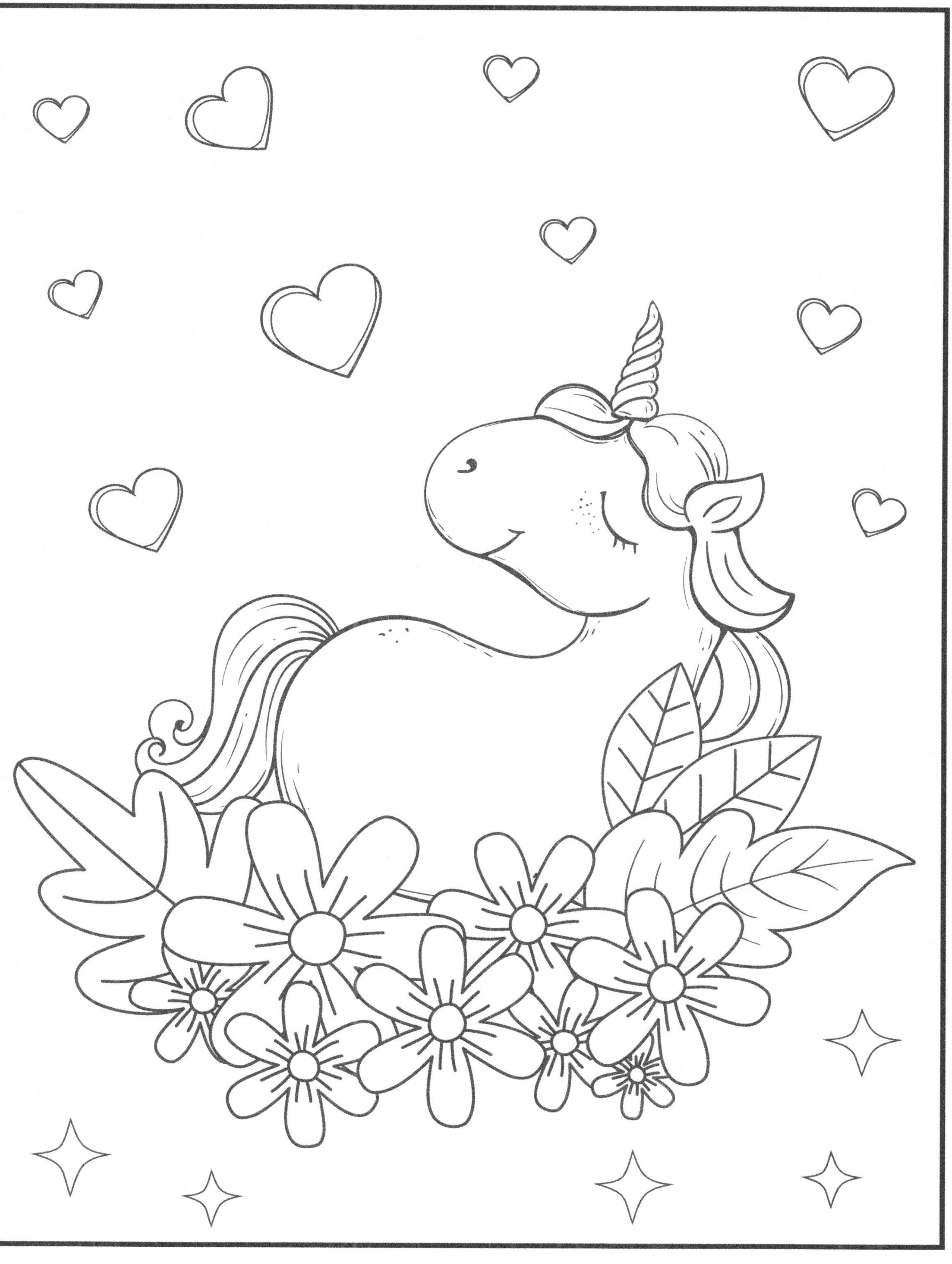

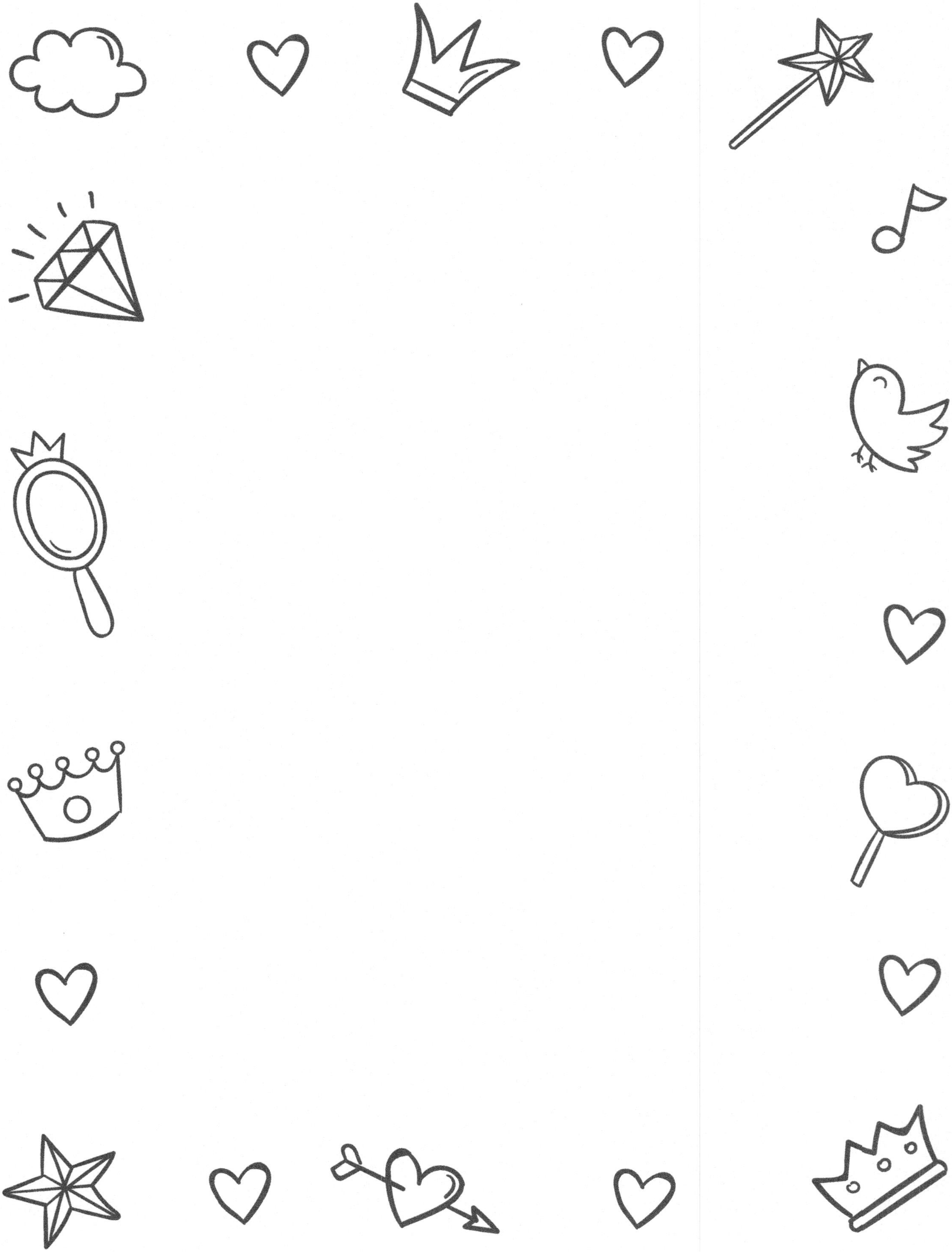

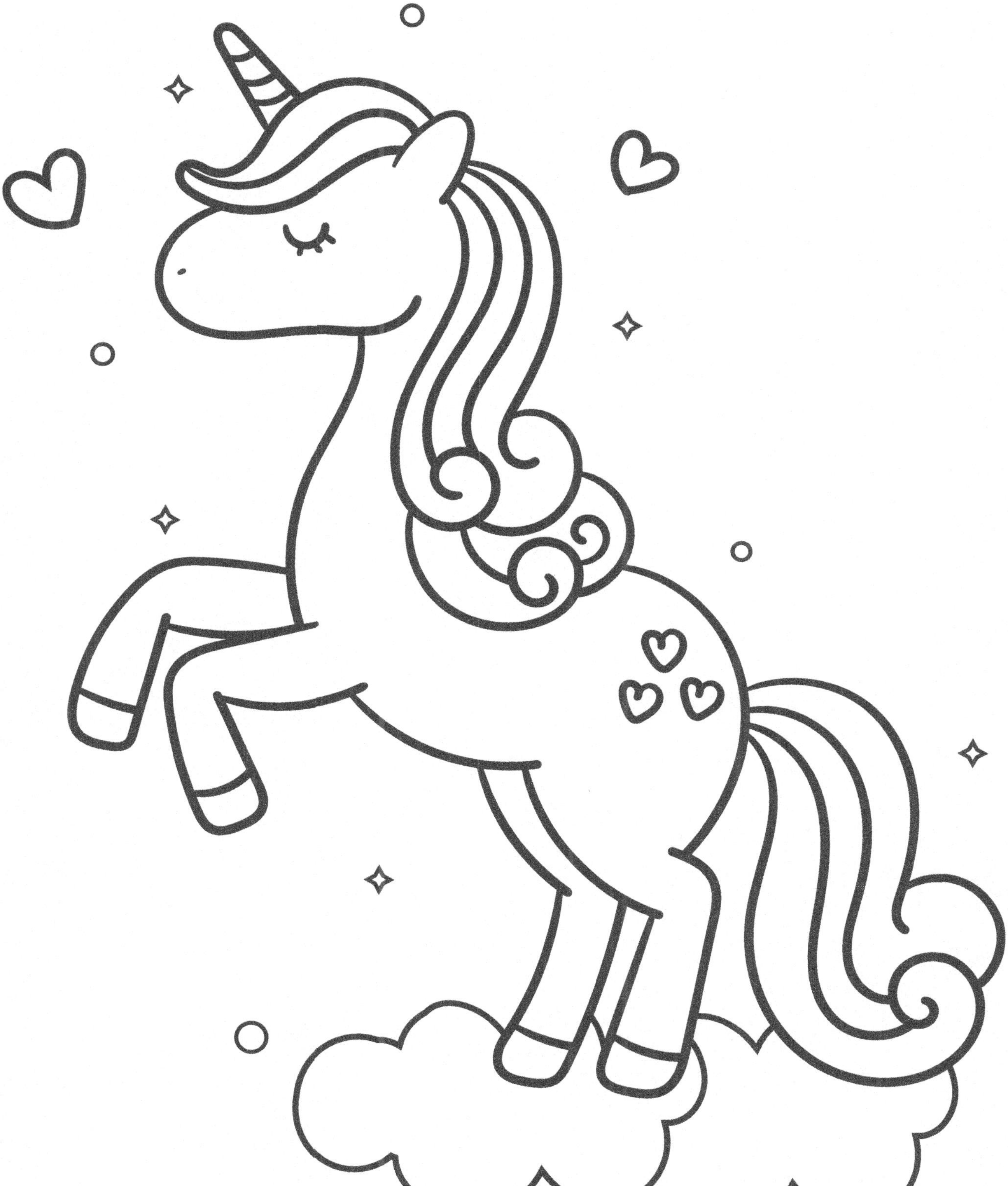

MAGICAL BIG SISTER!

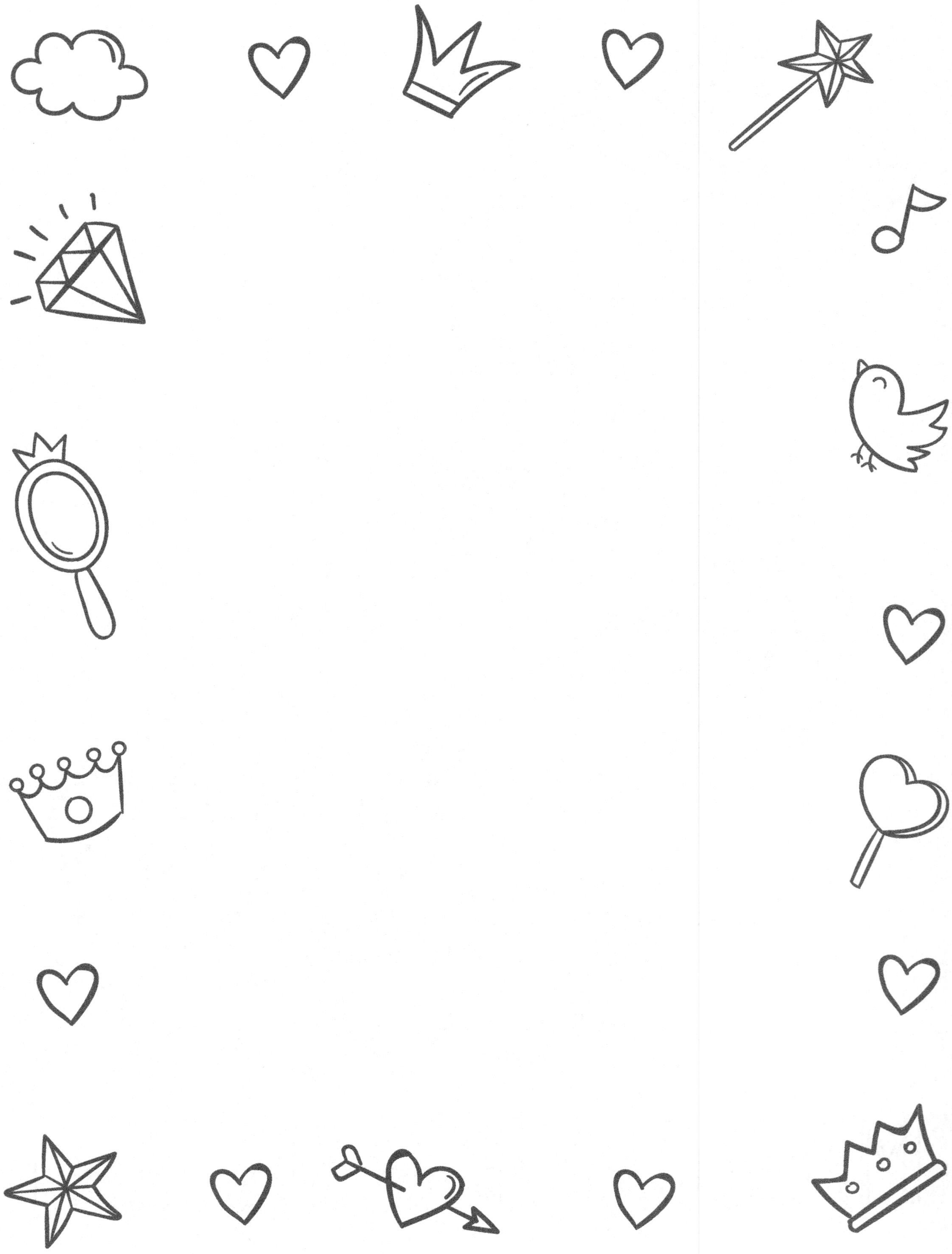

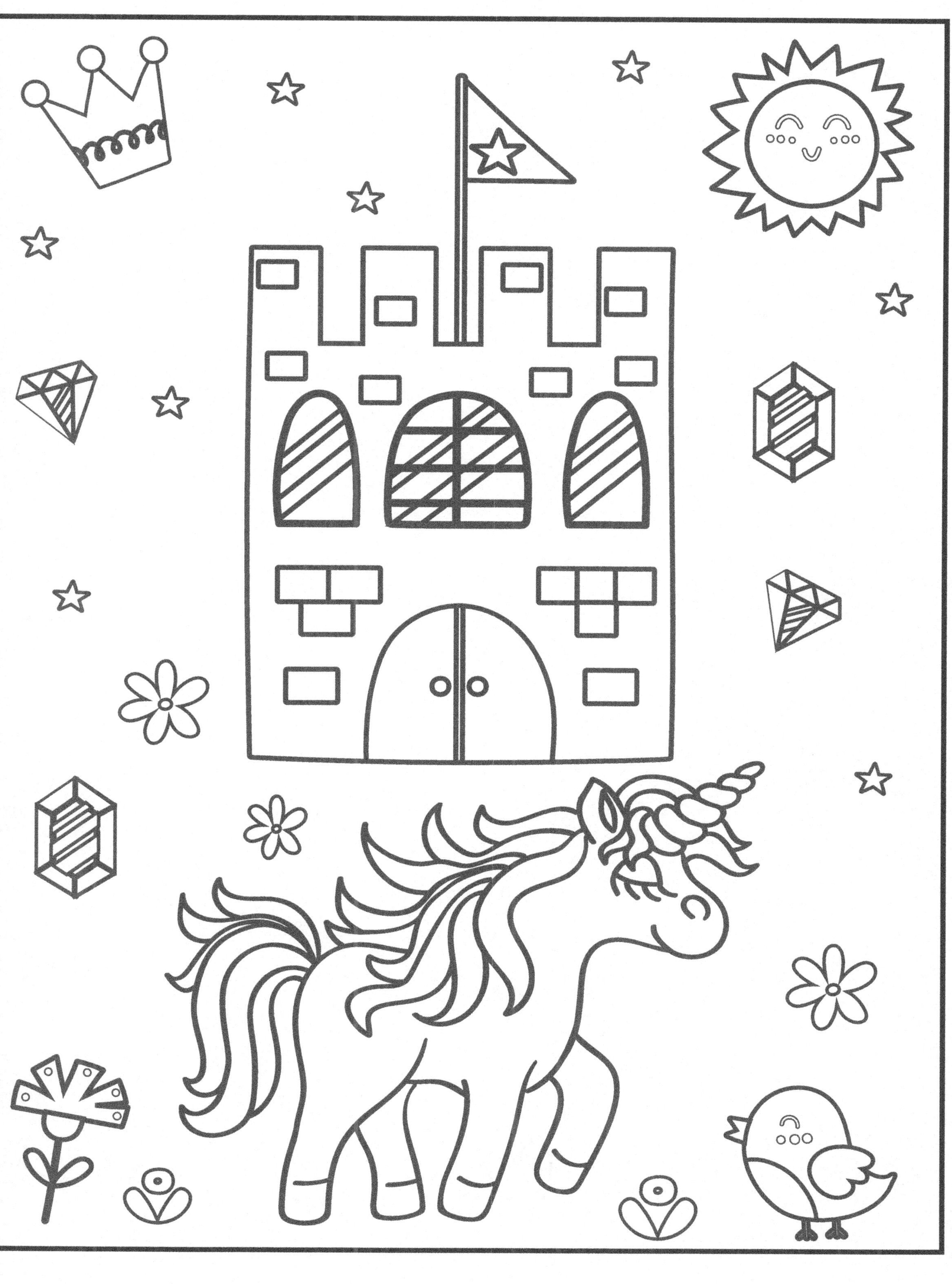

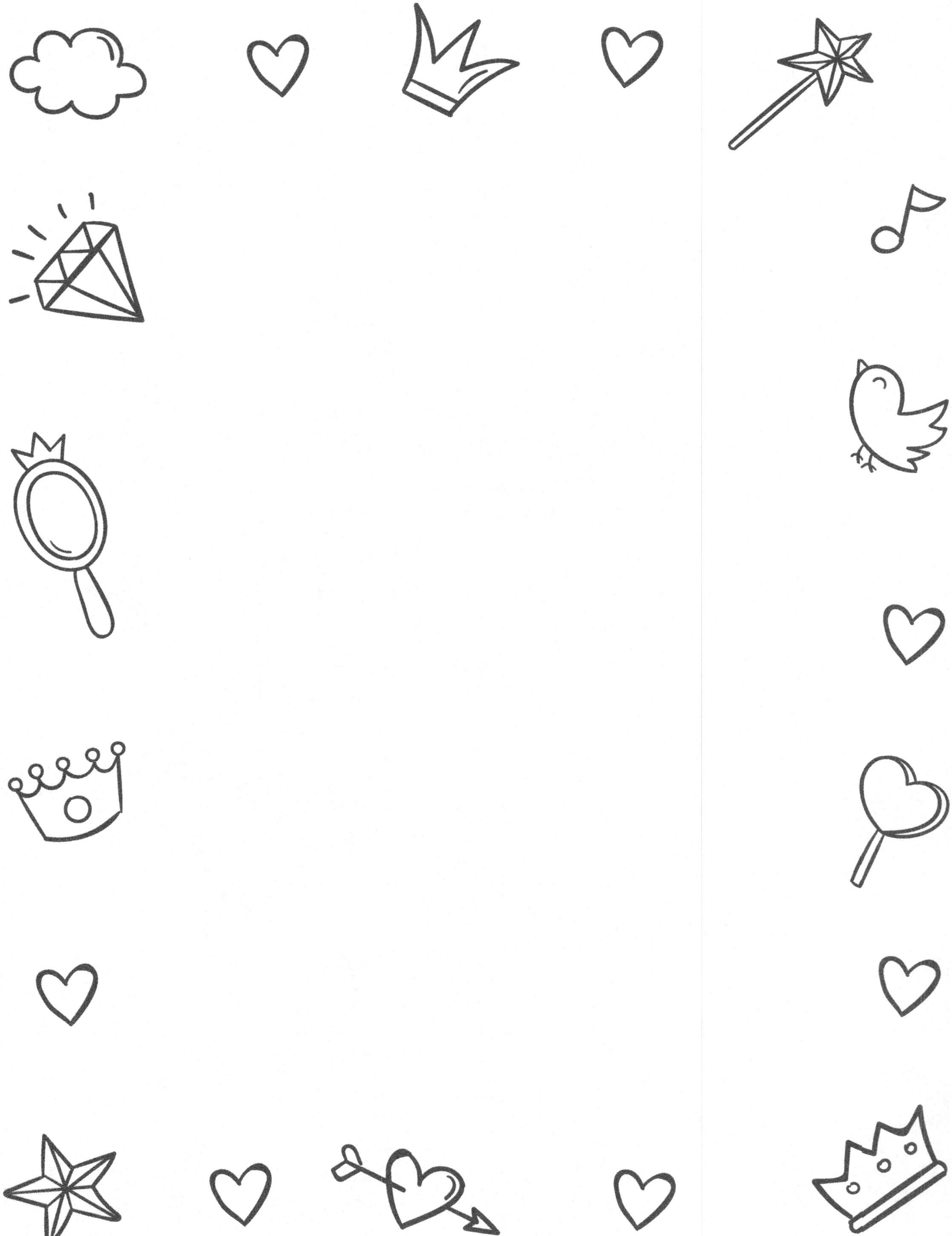

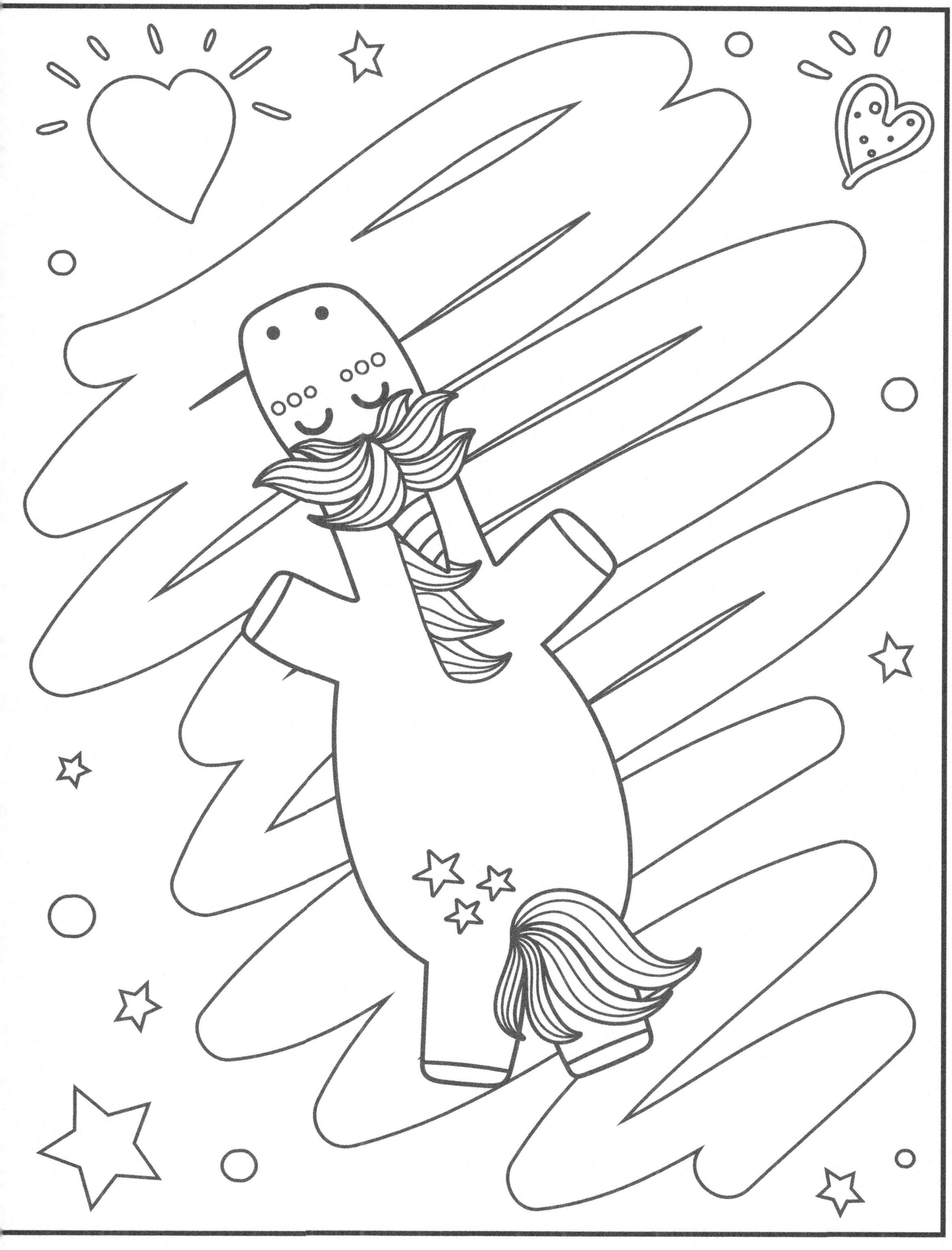

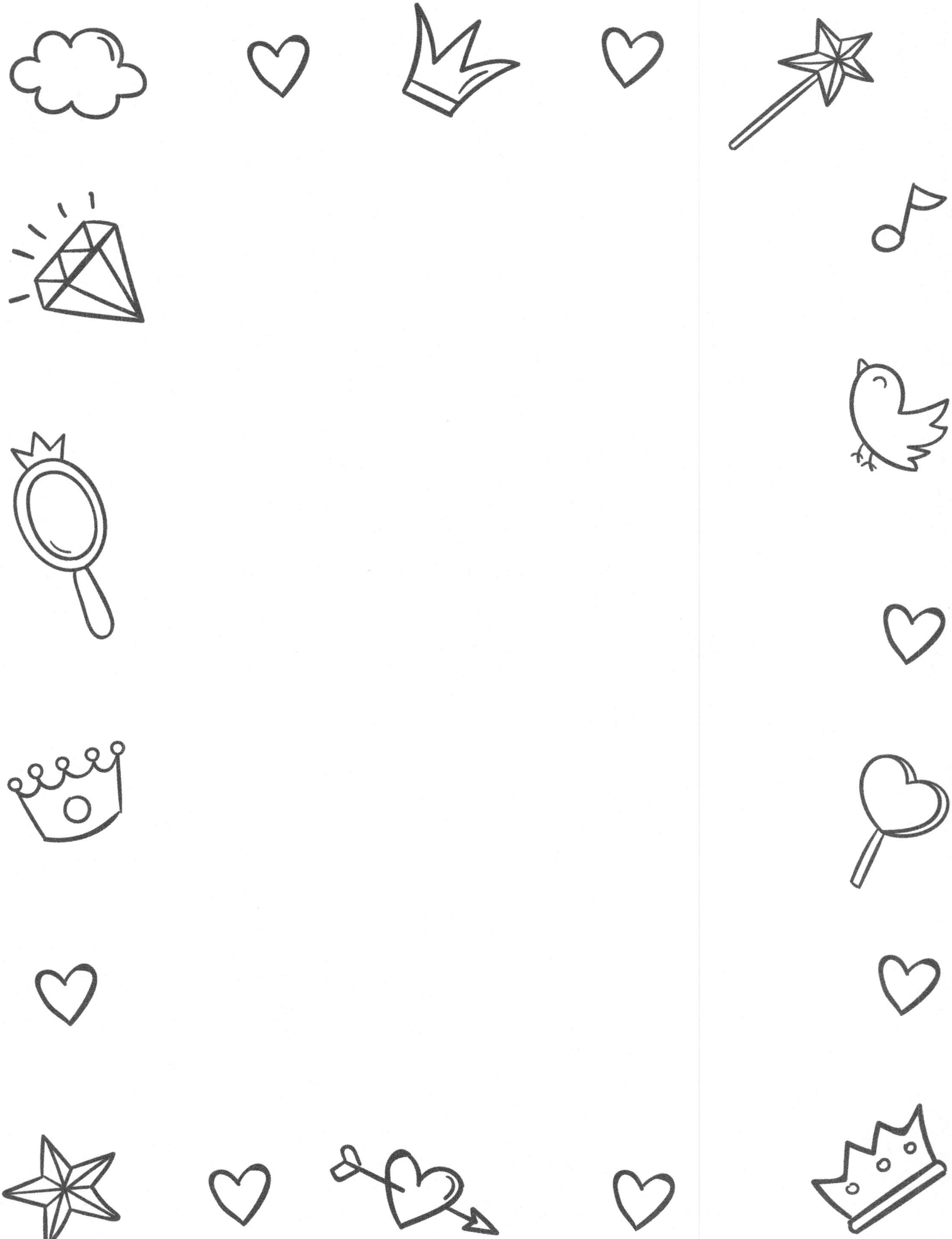

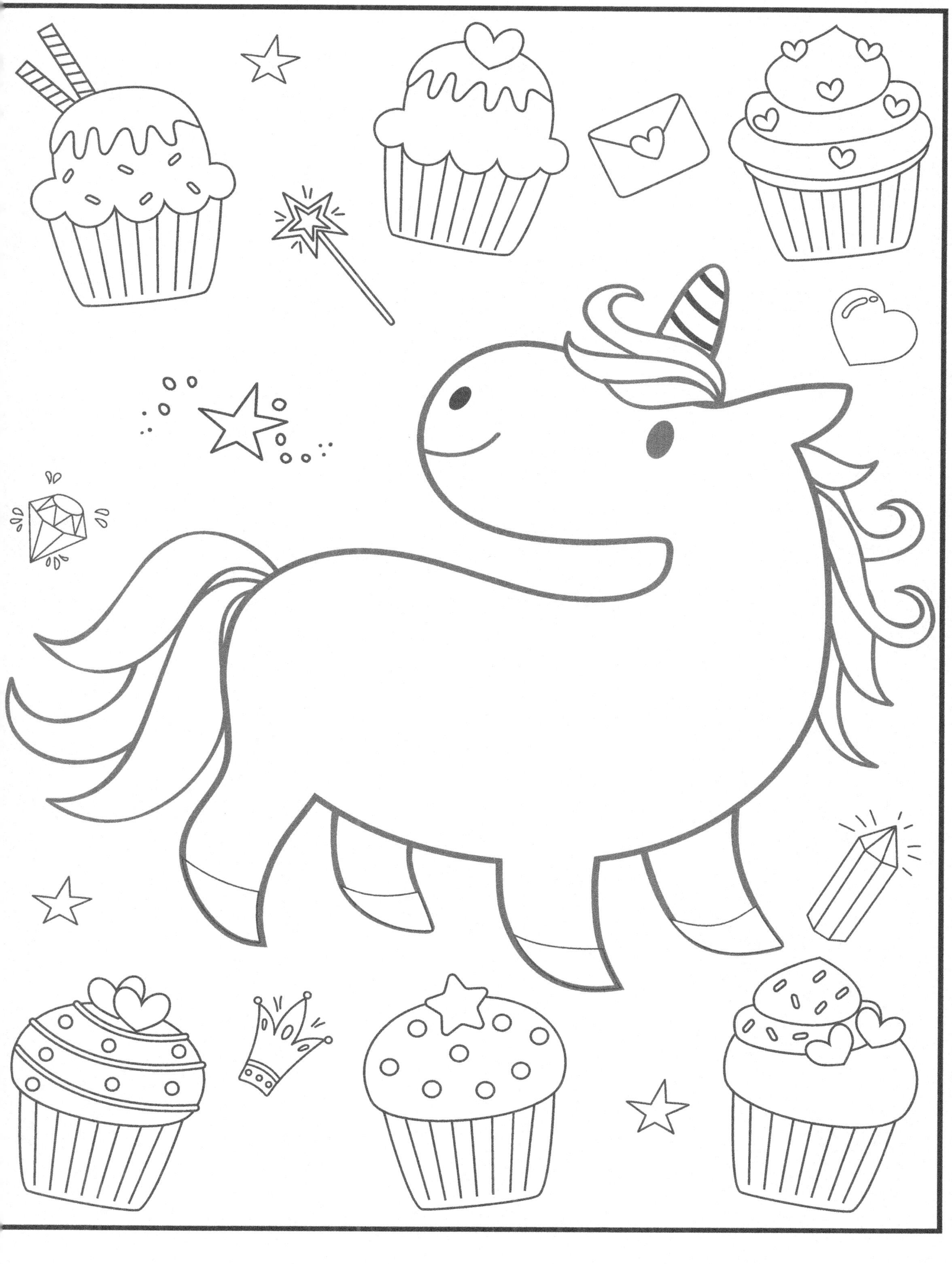

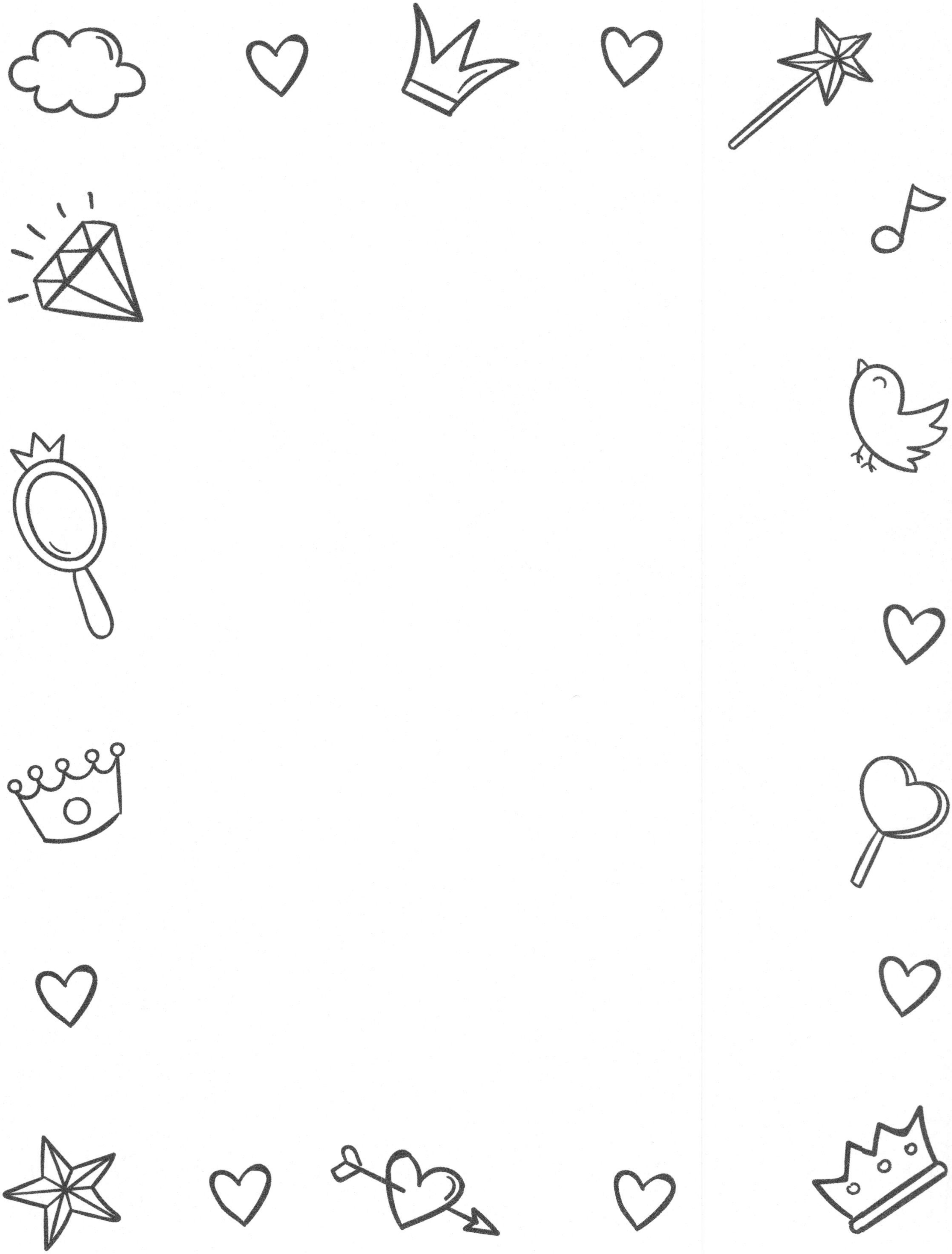

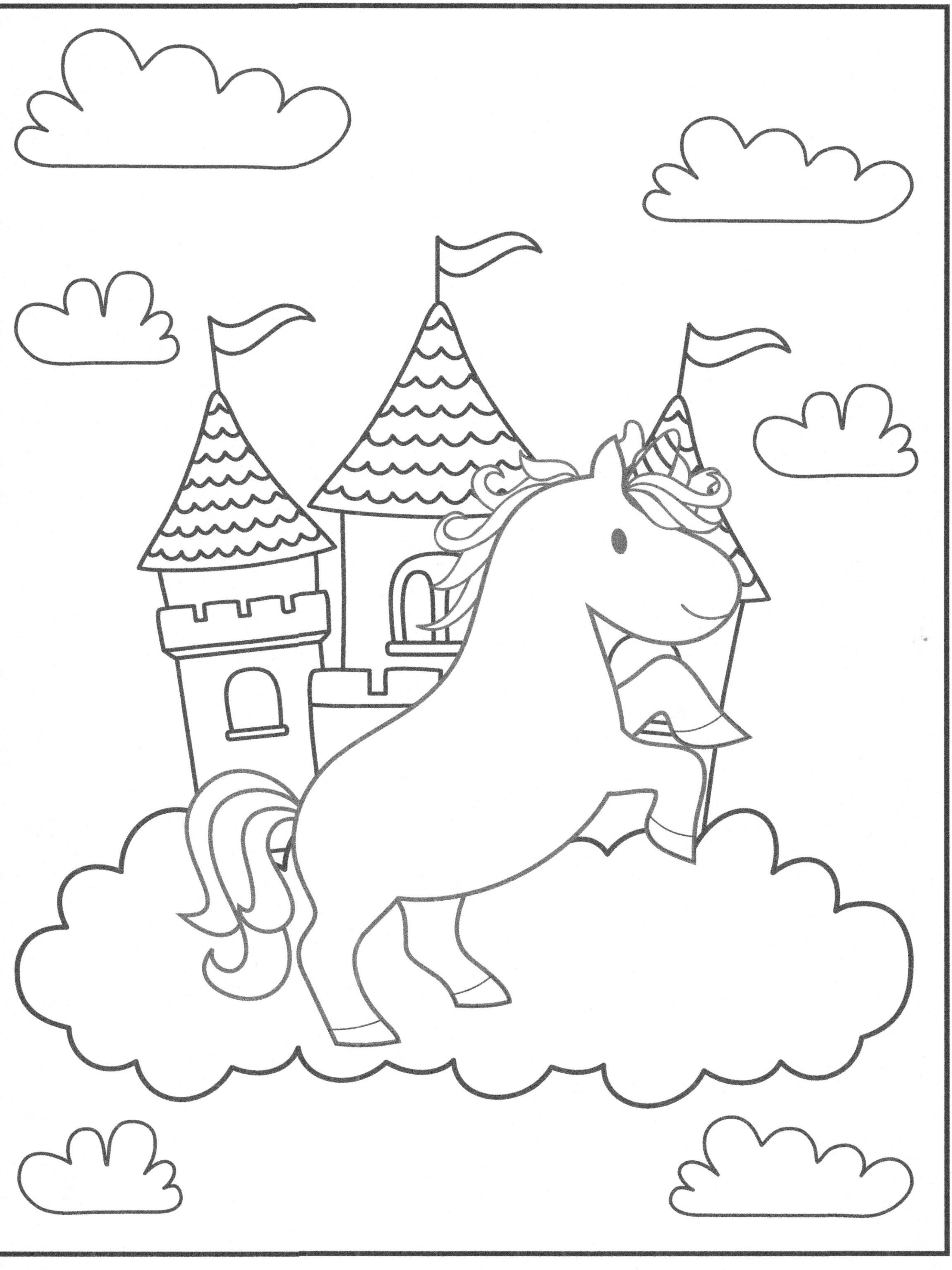

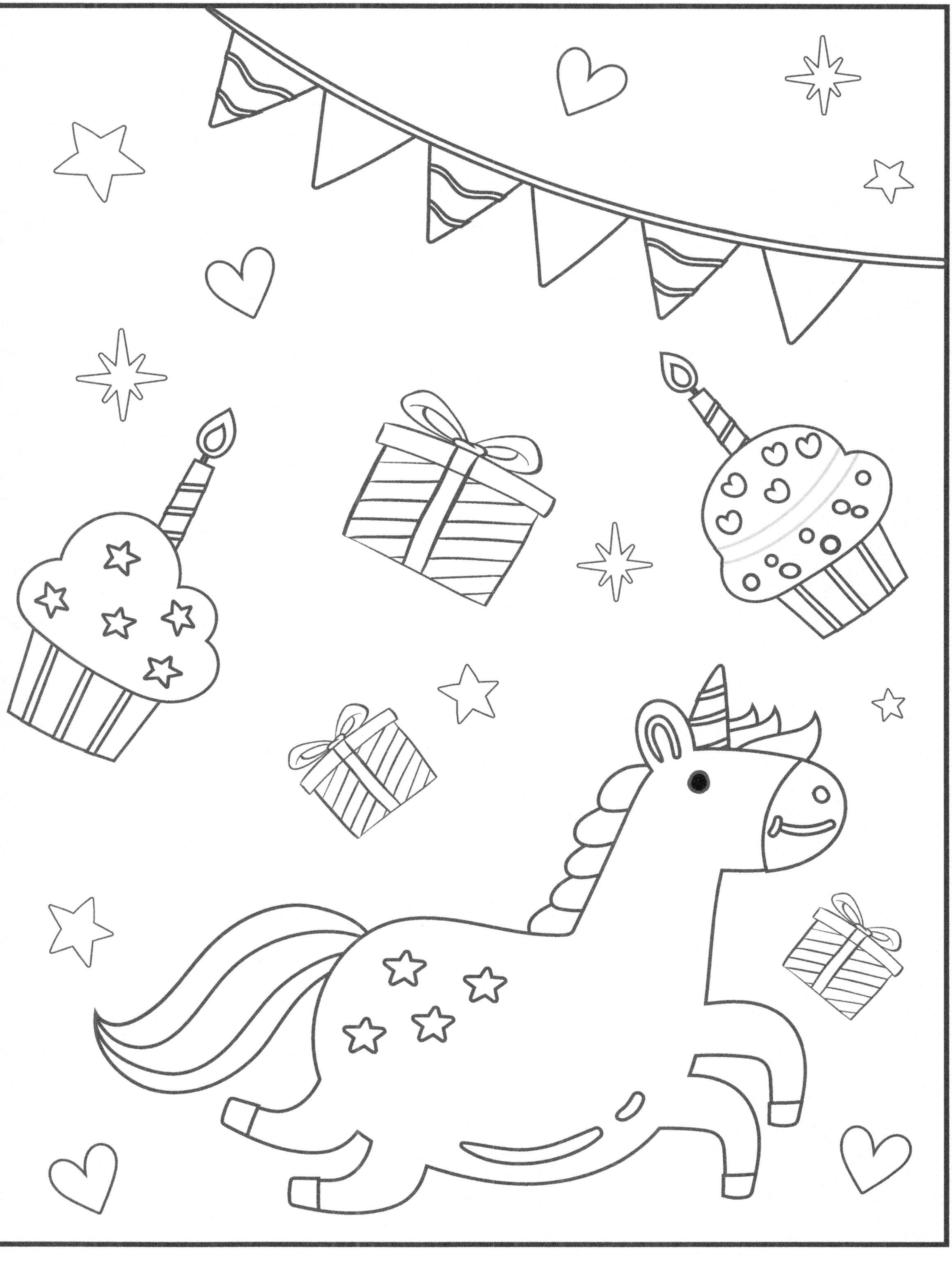

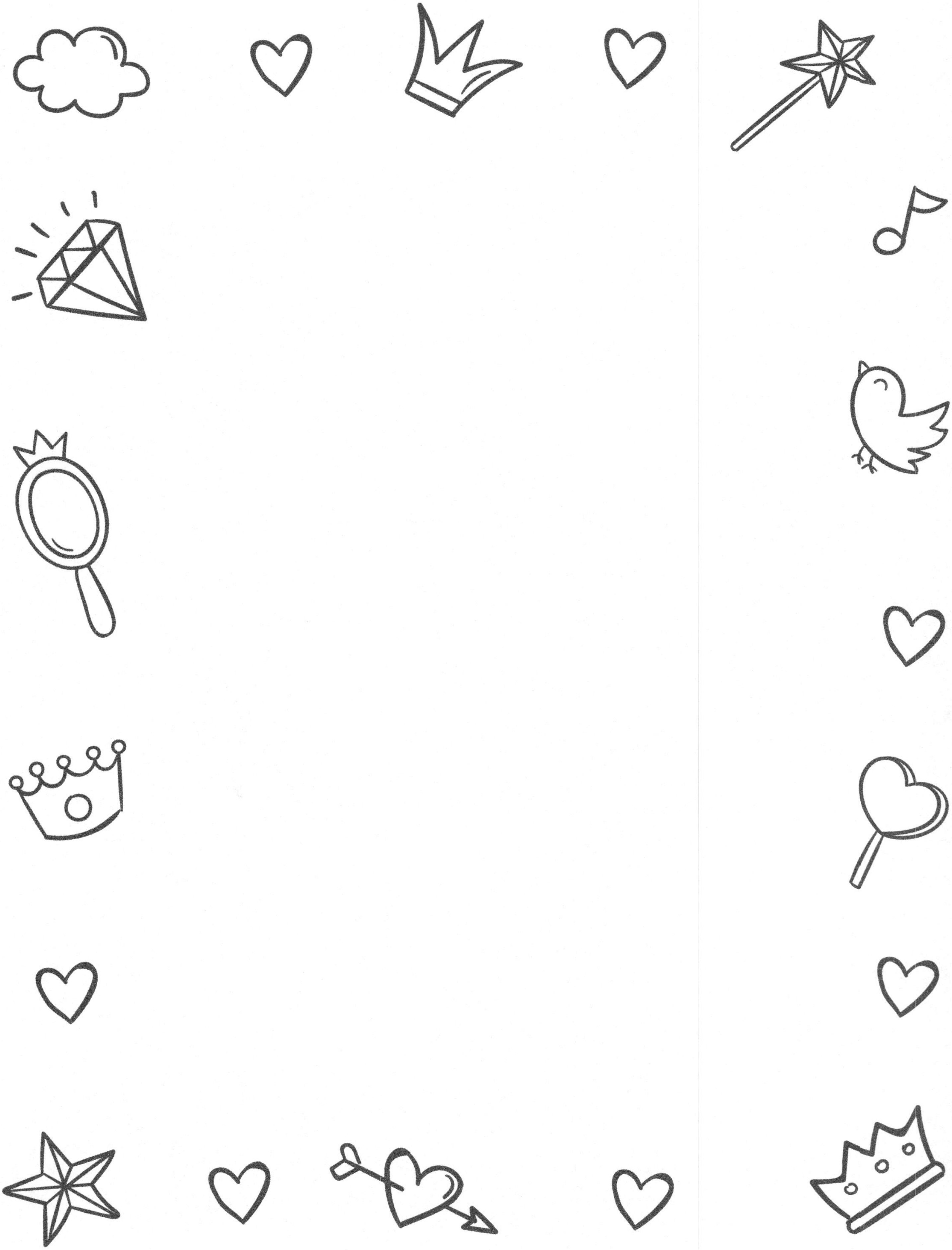

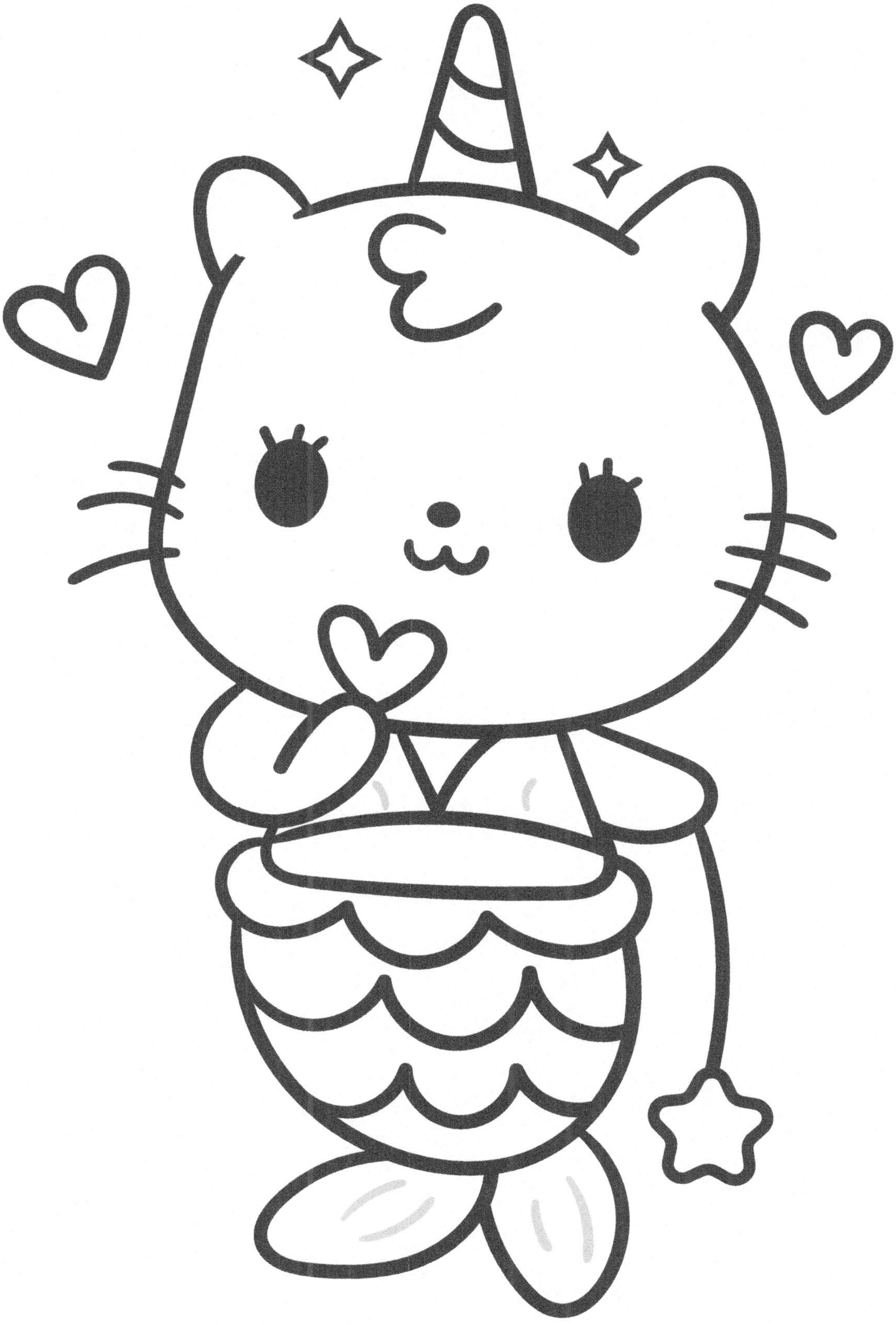

BEAUTIFUL BIG SISTER !

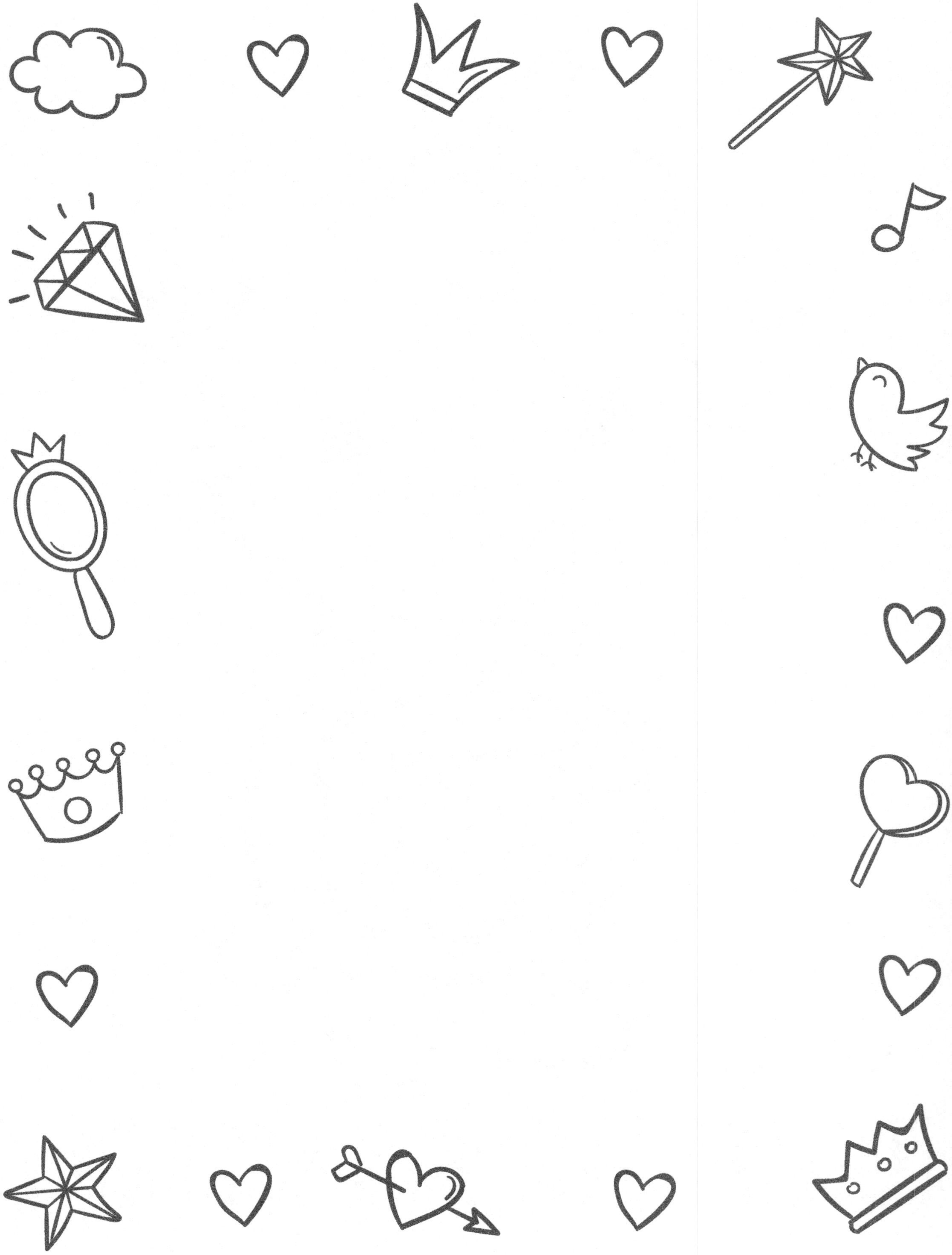

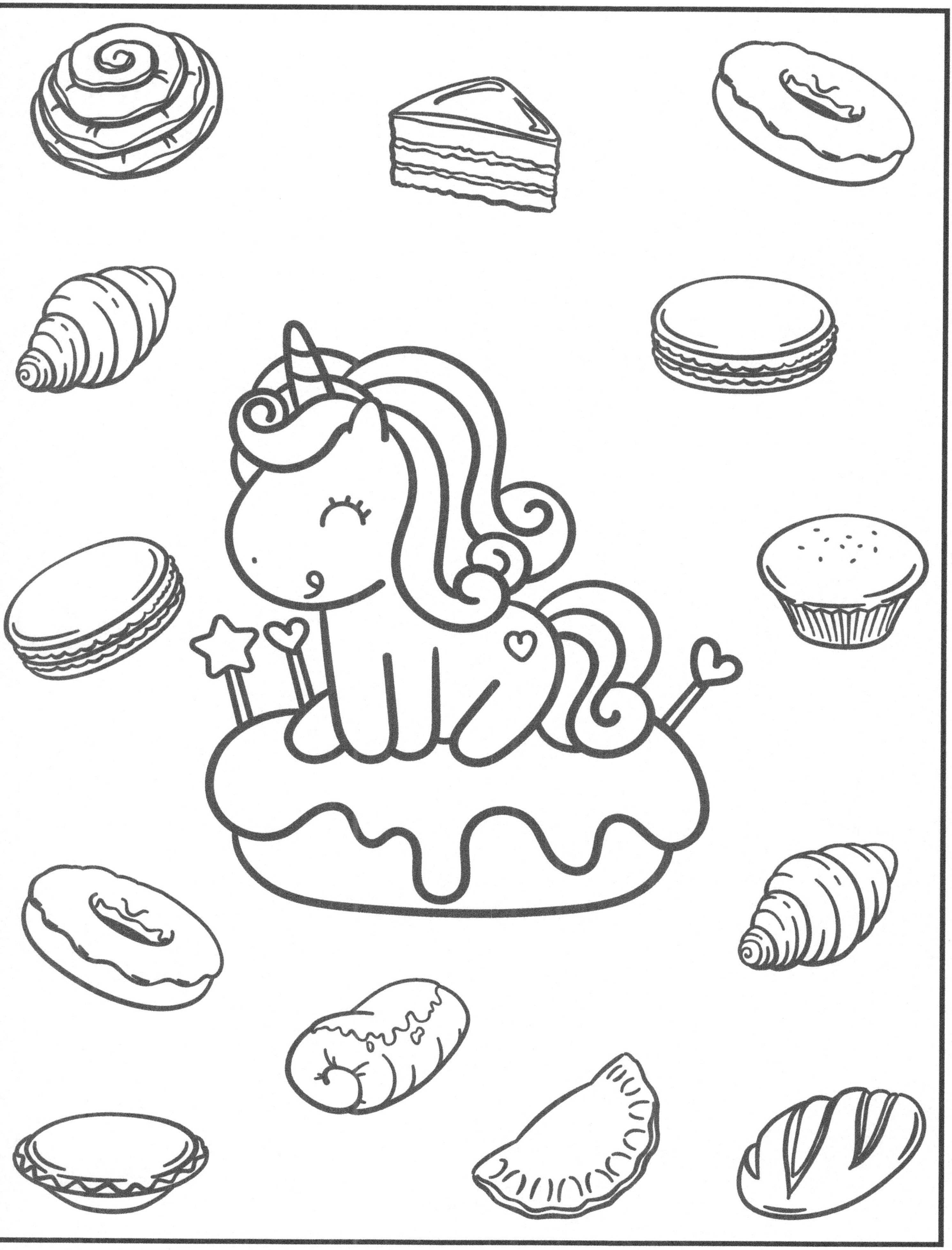

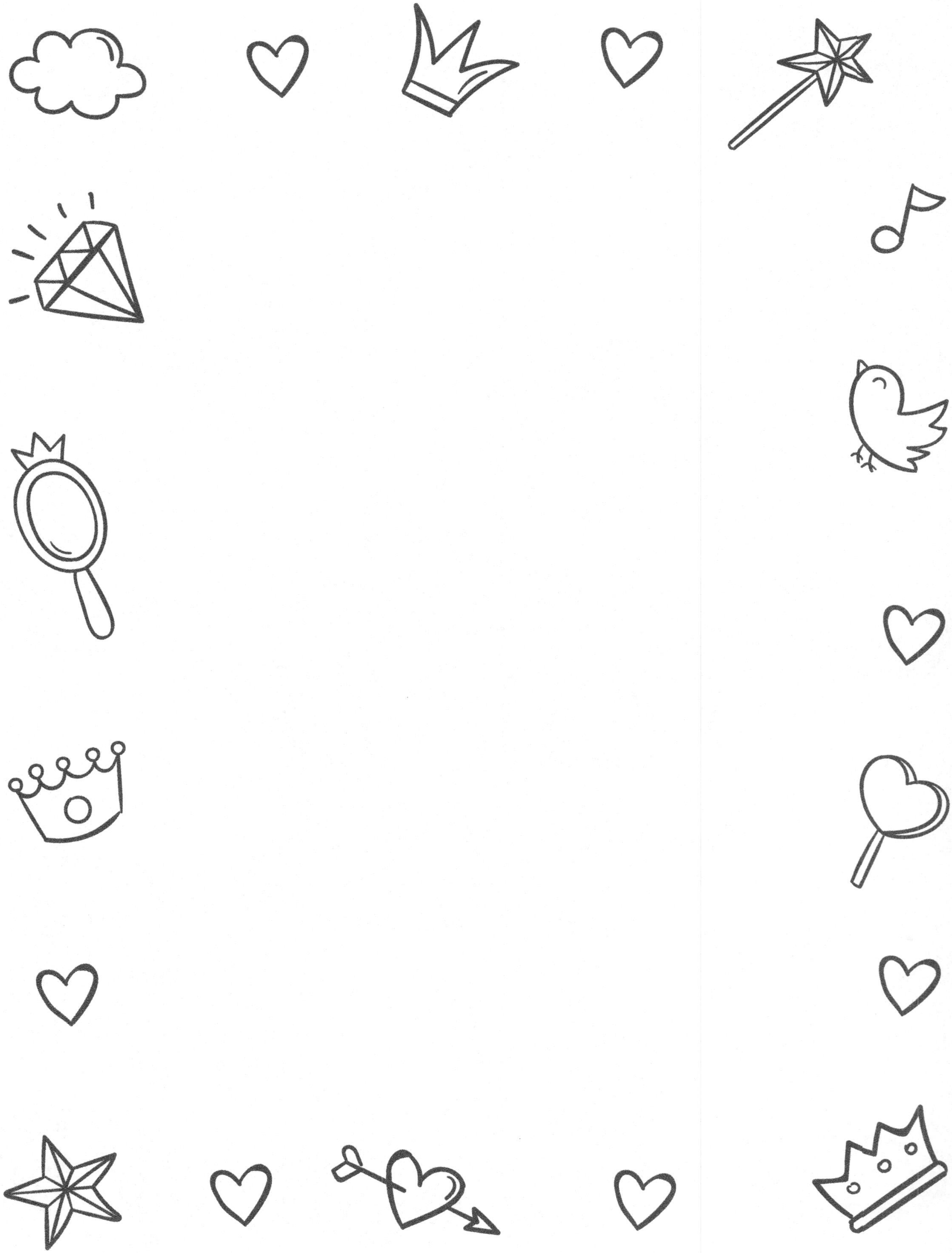

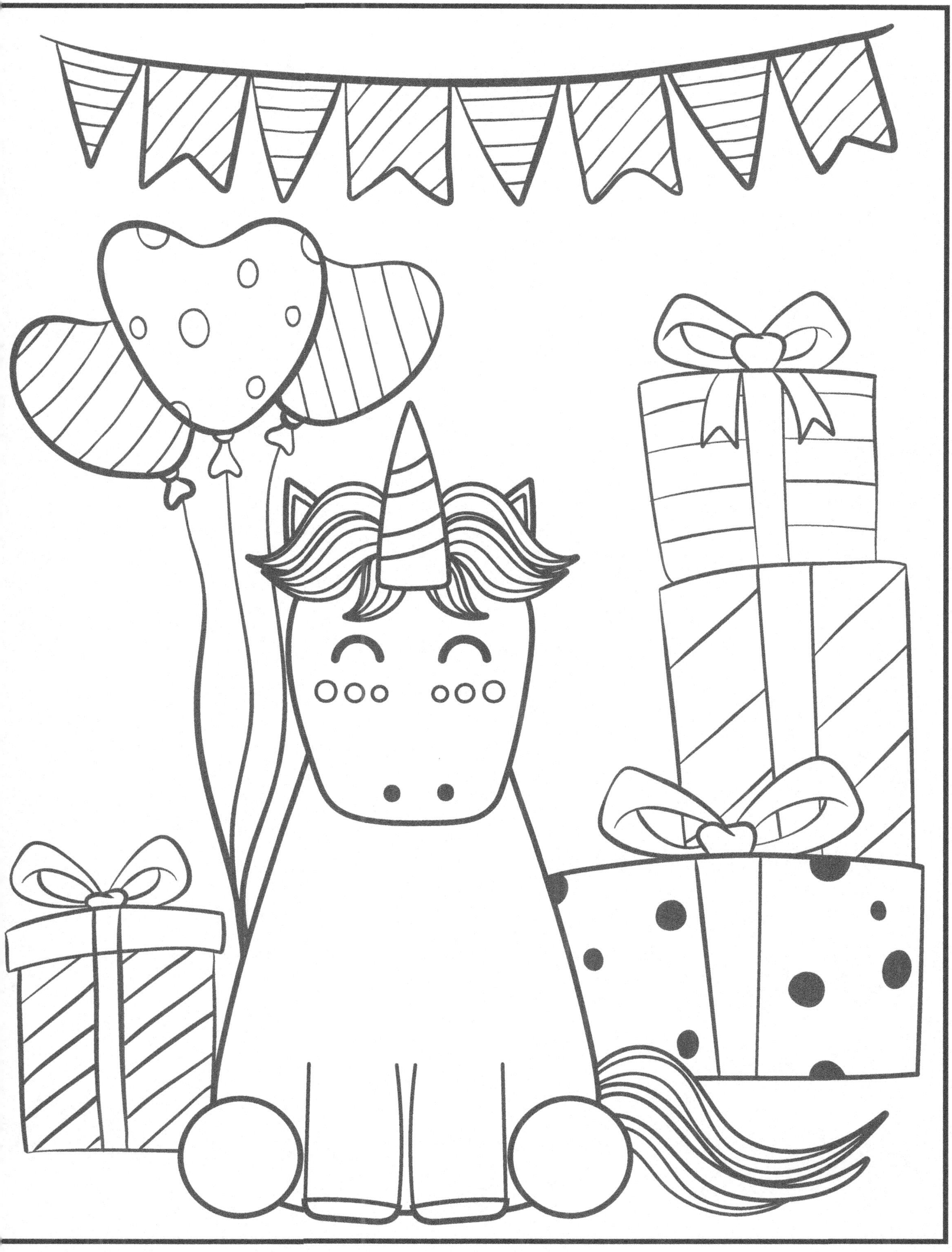

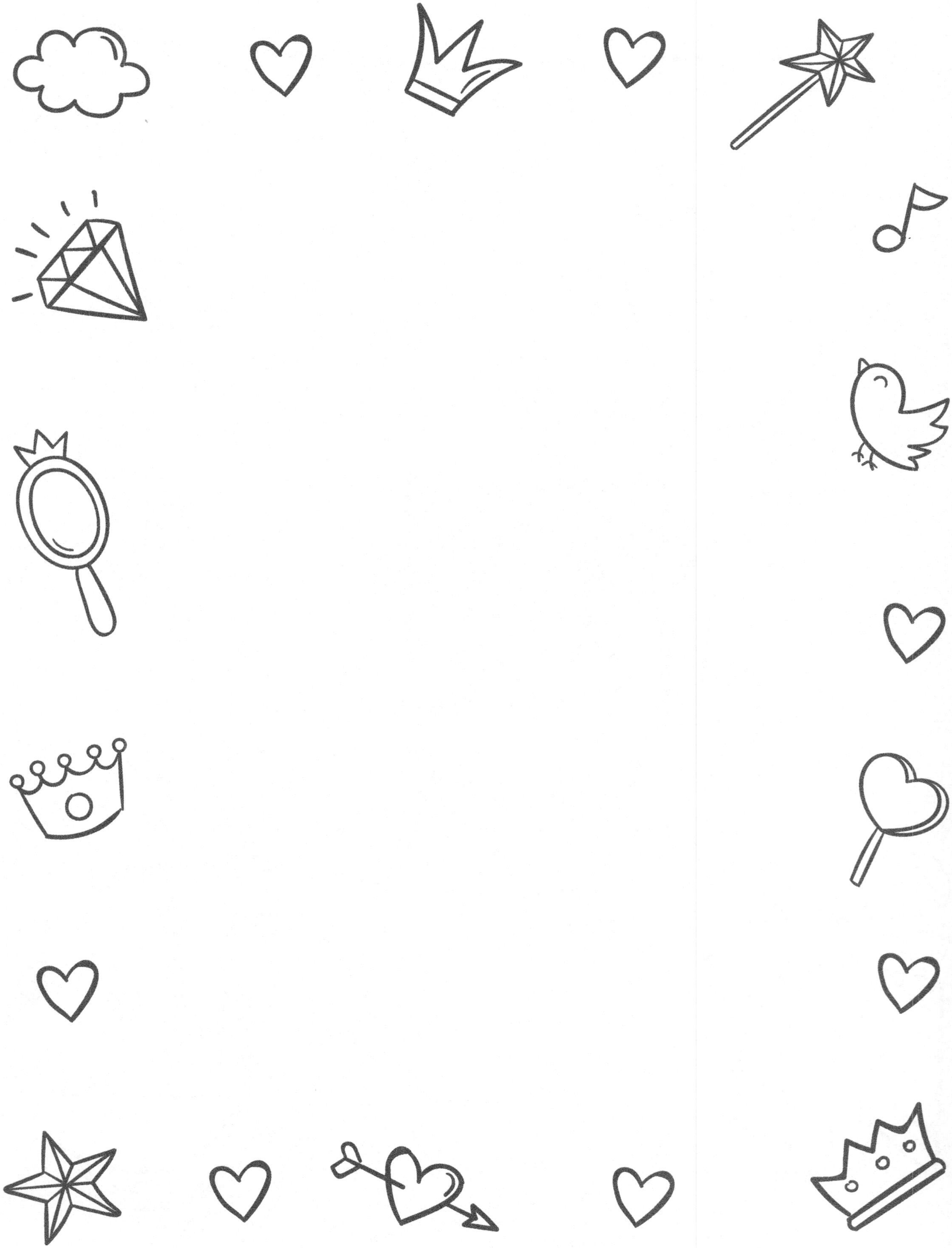

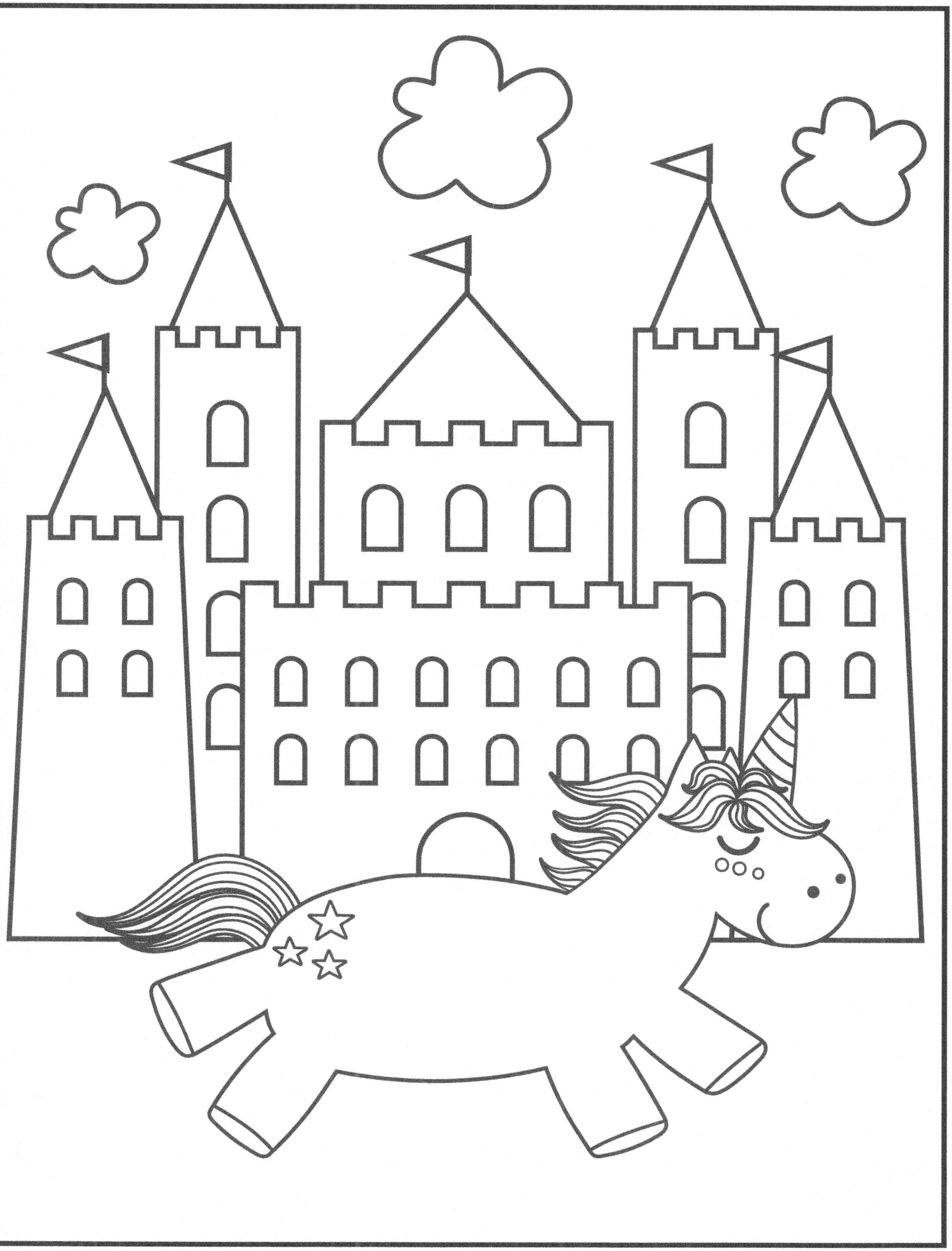

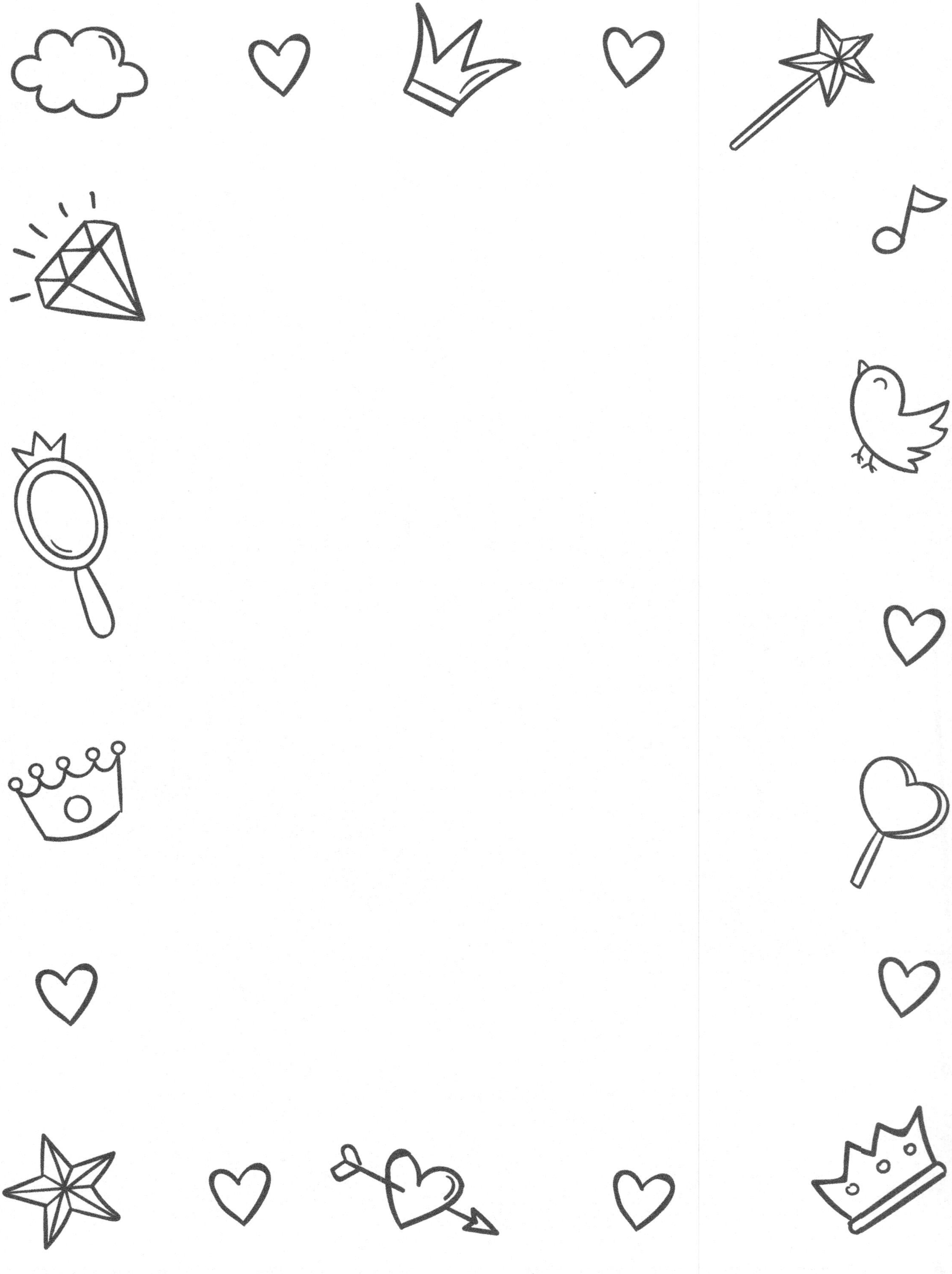

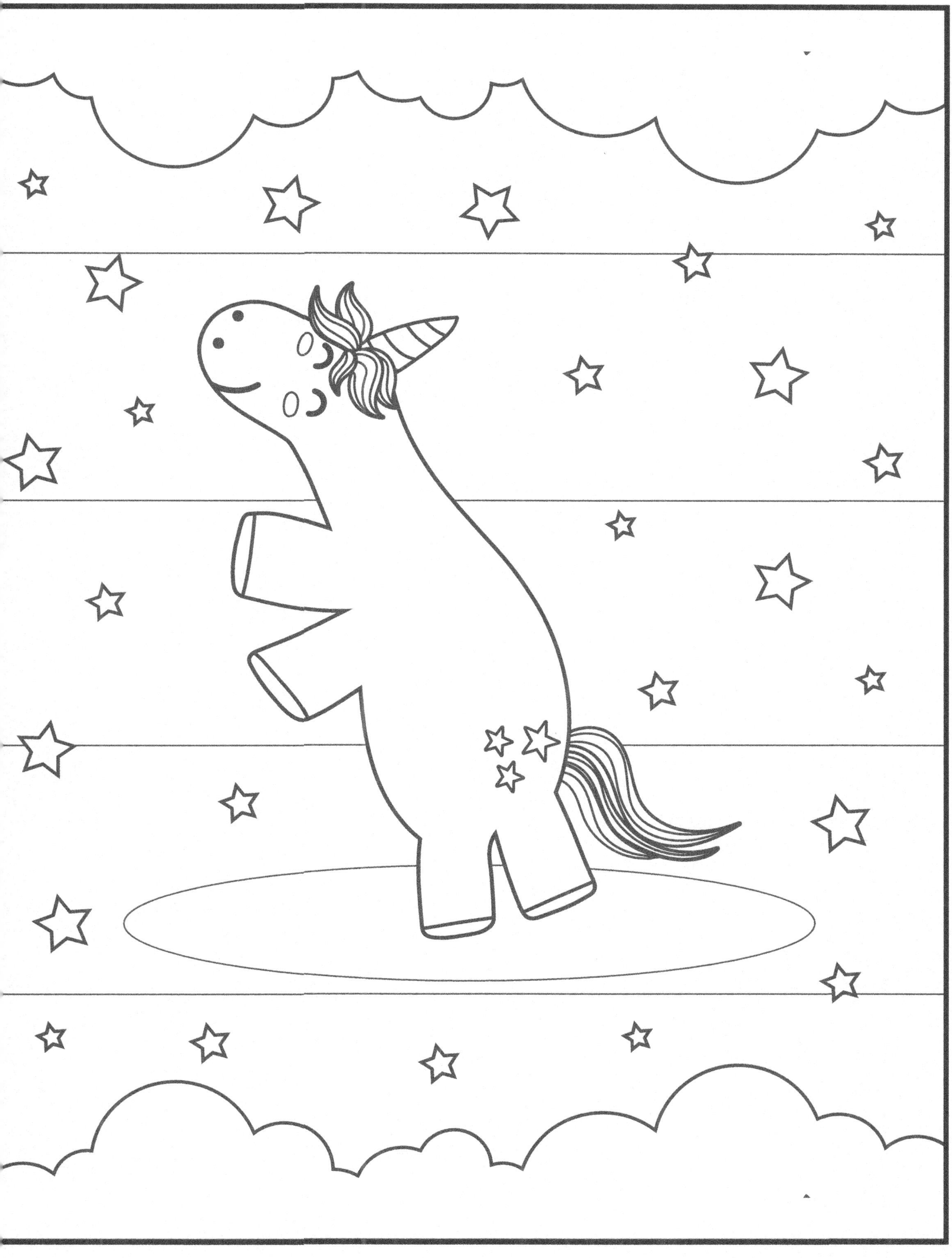

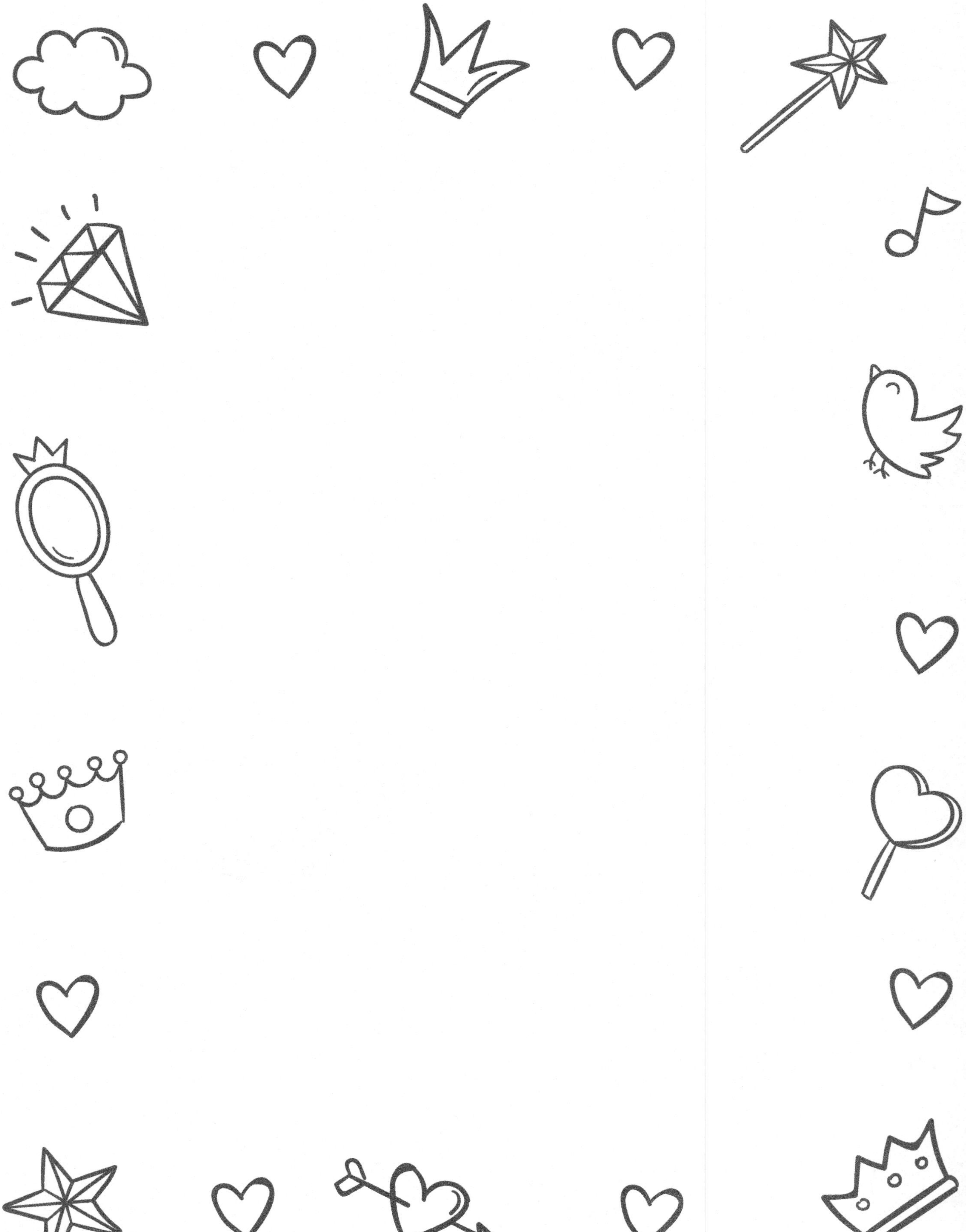

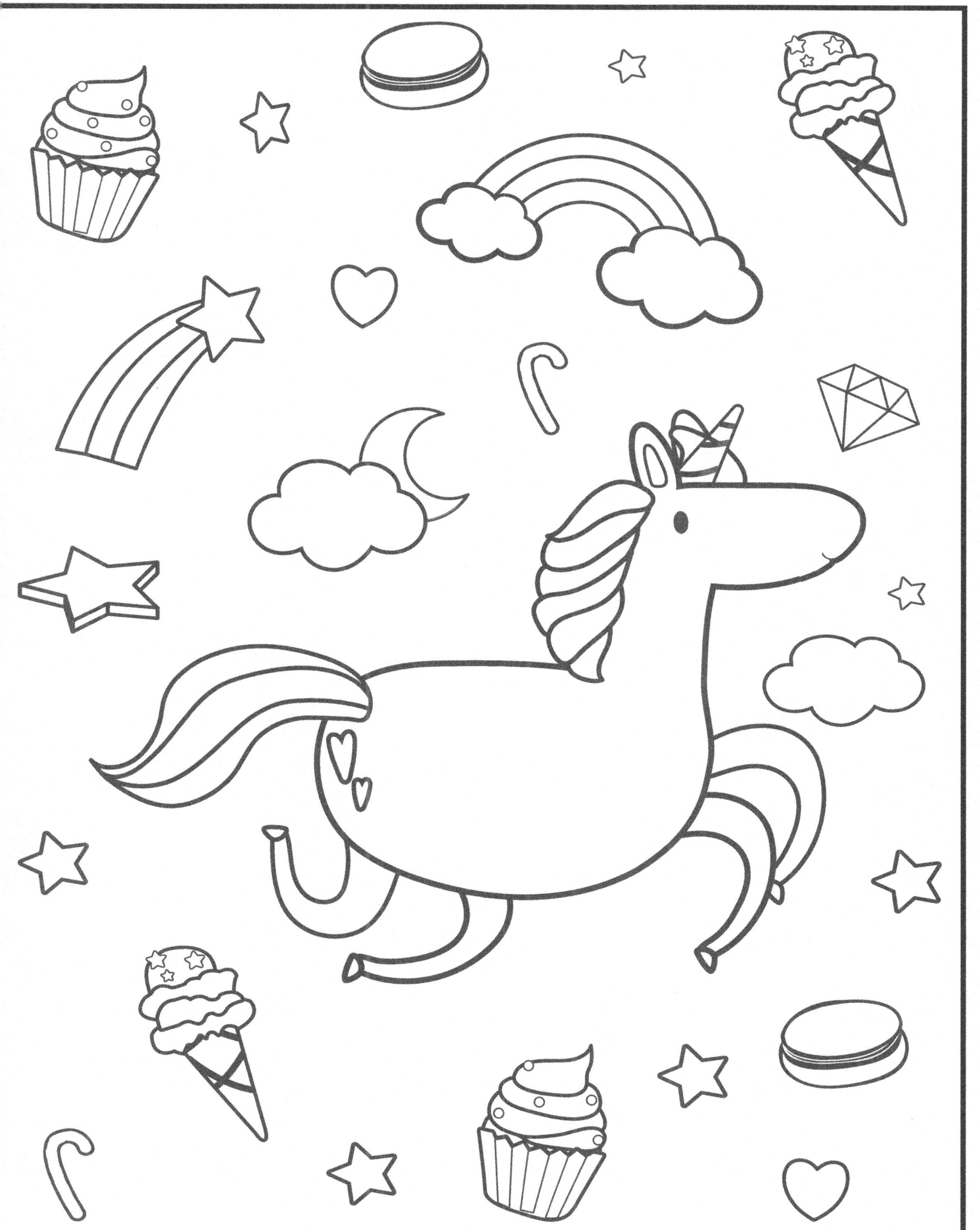

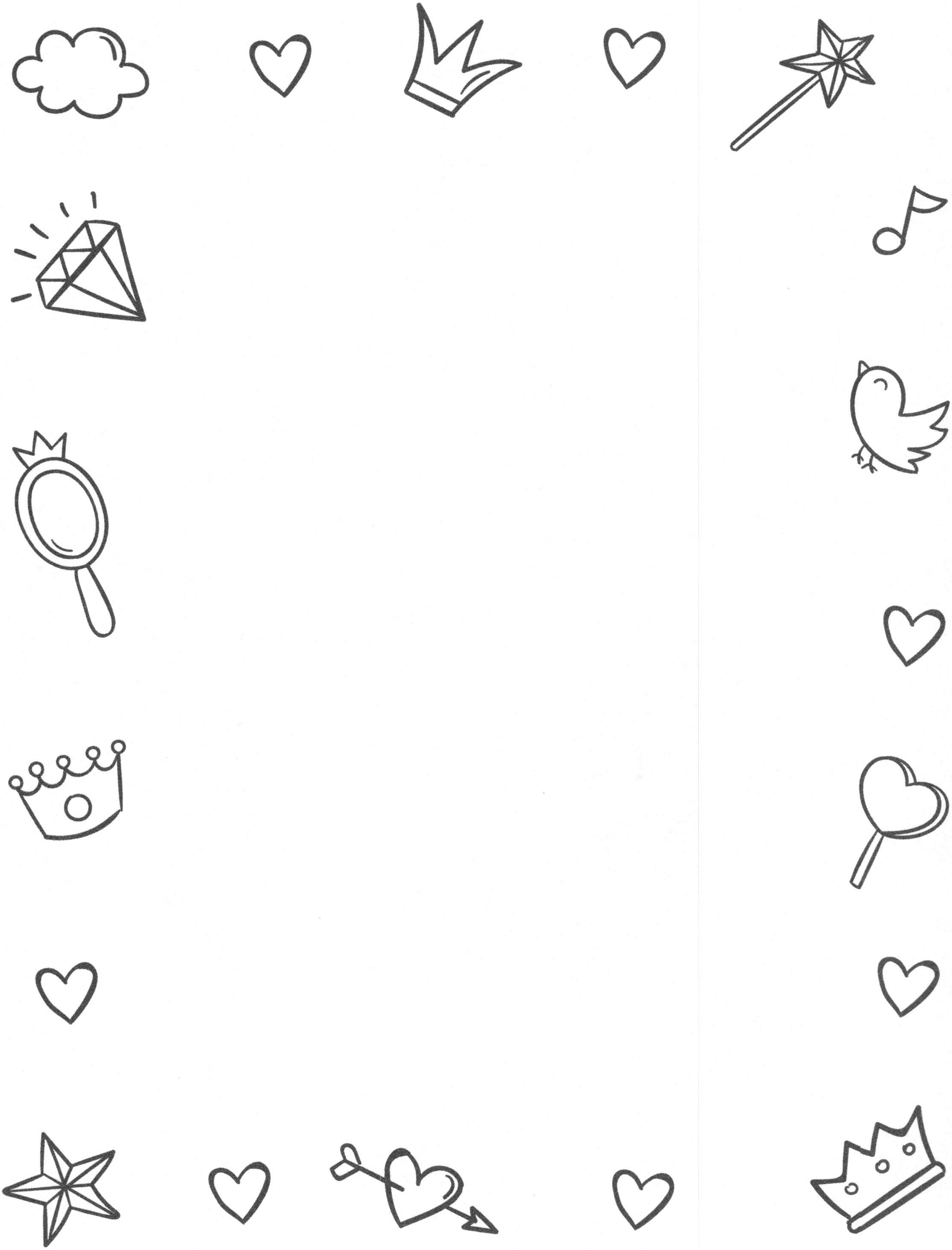

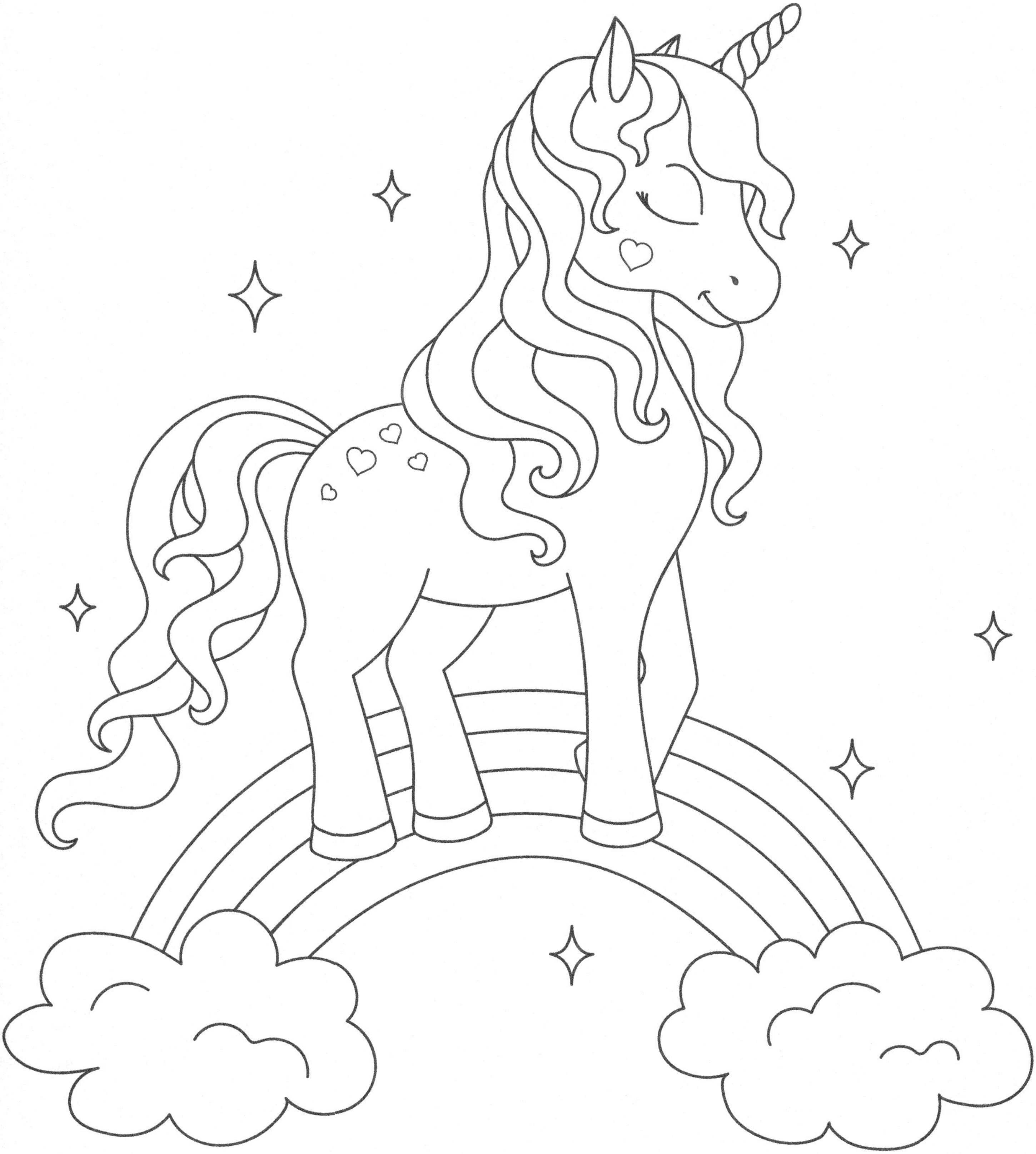

FABULOUS BIG SISTER!

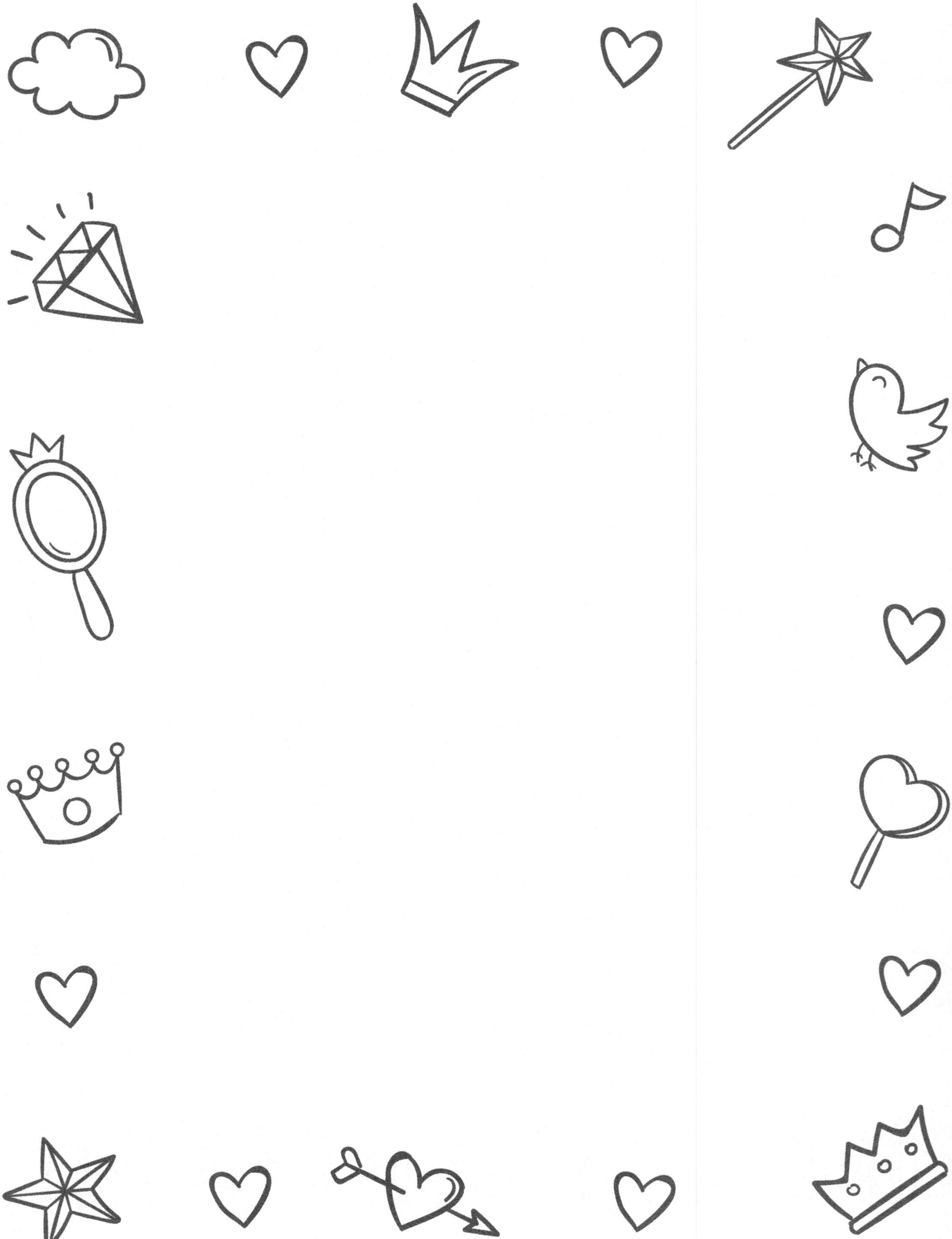

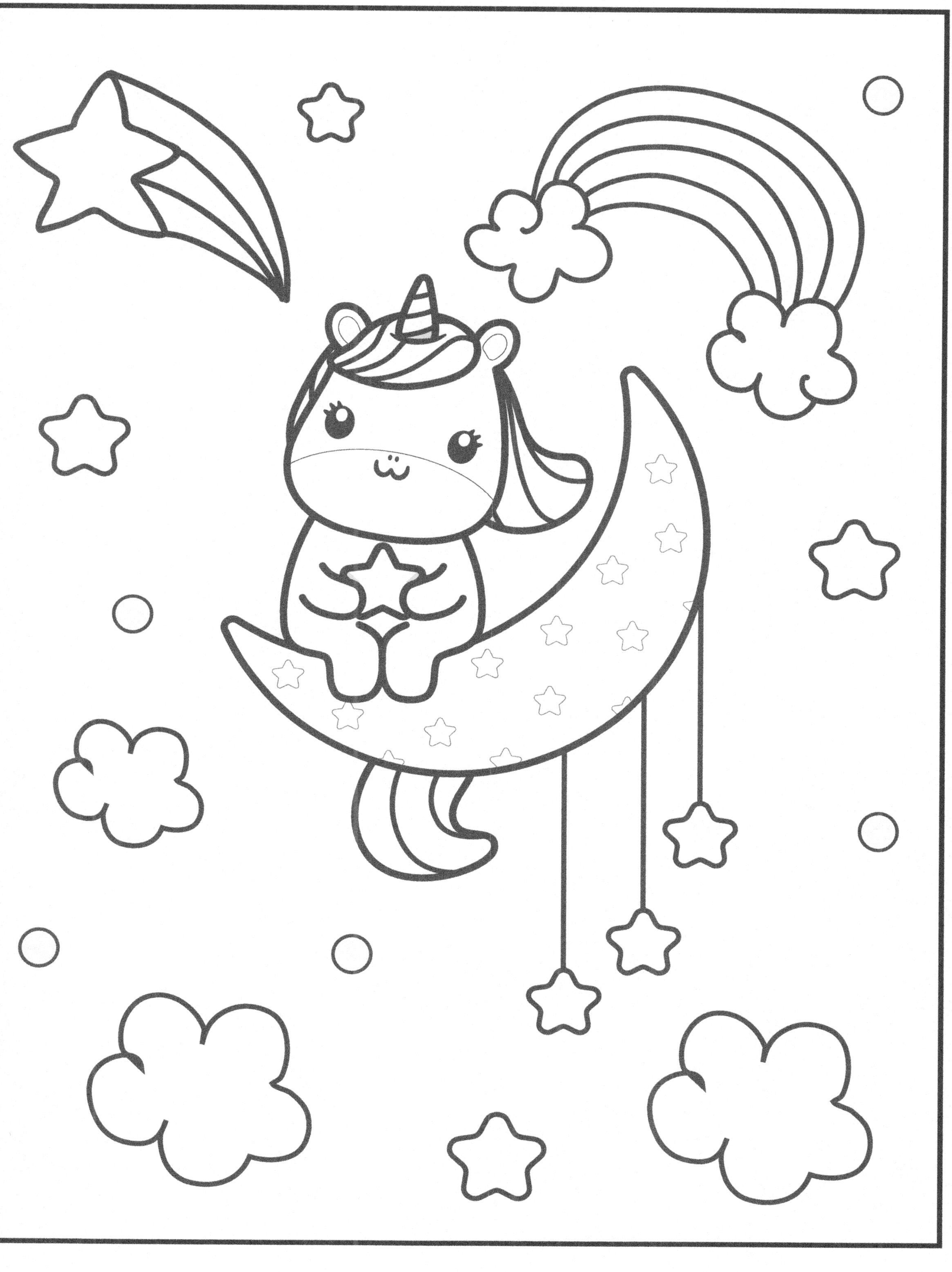

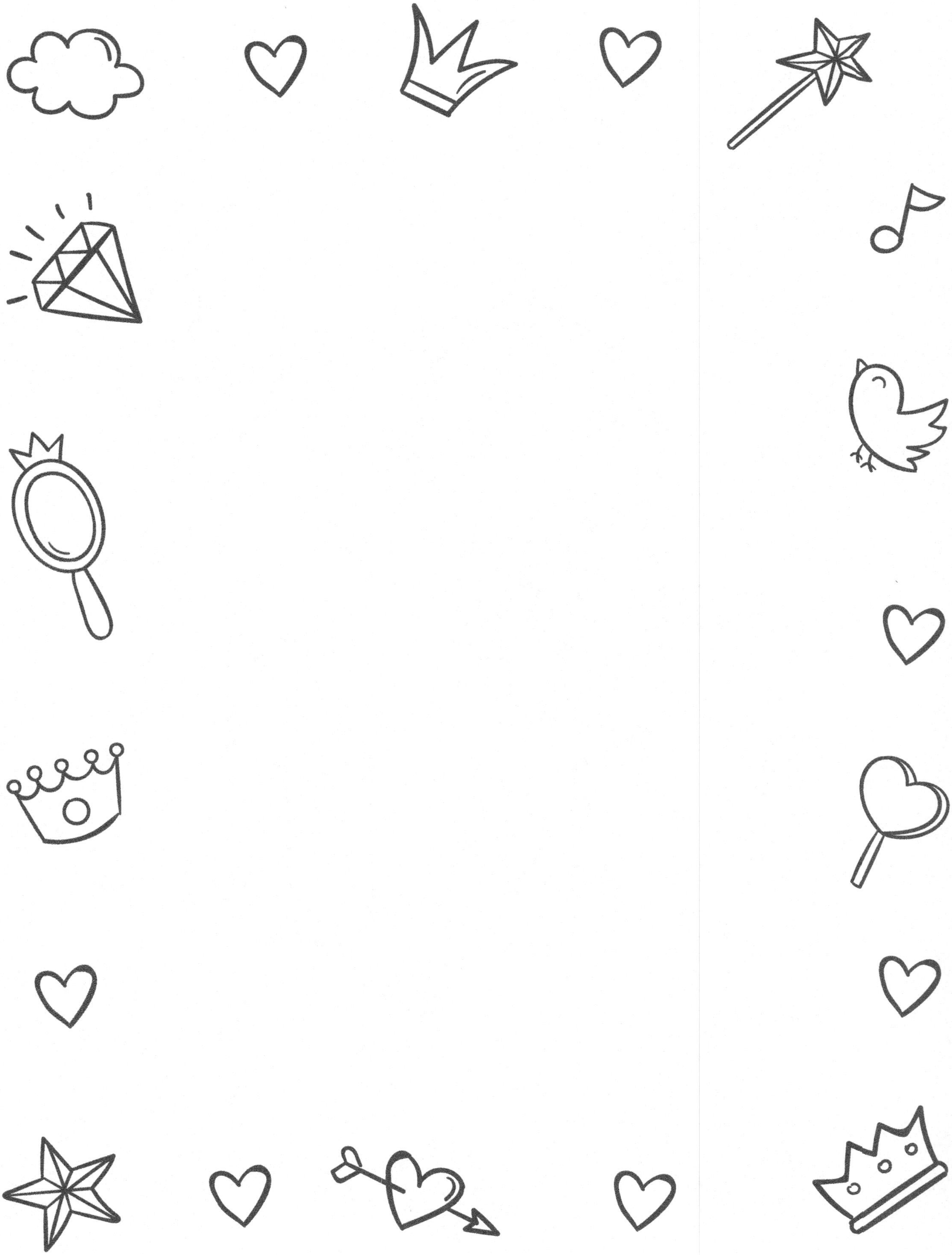

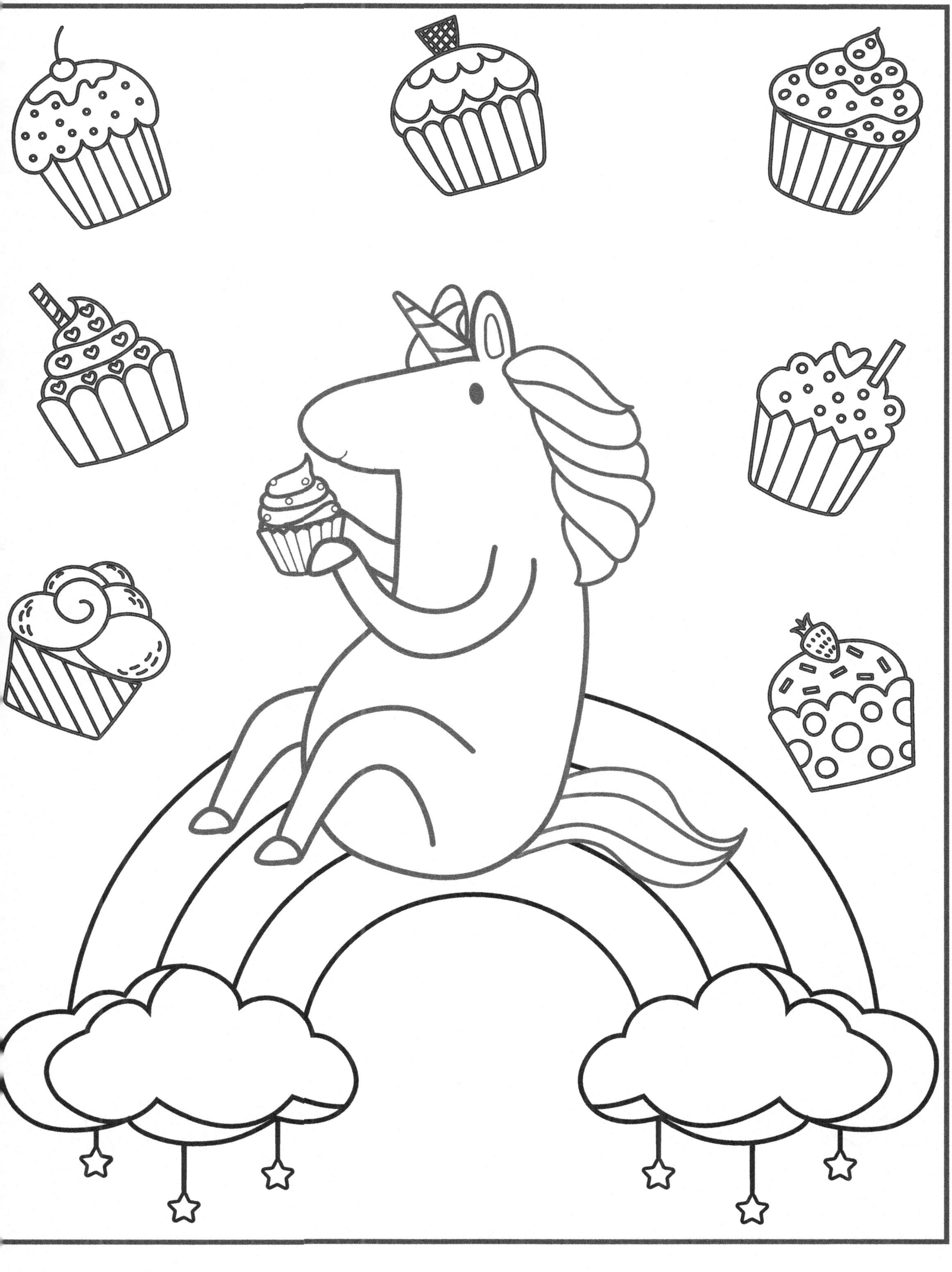

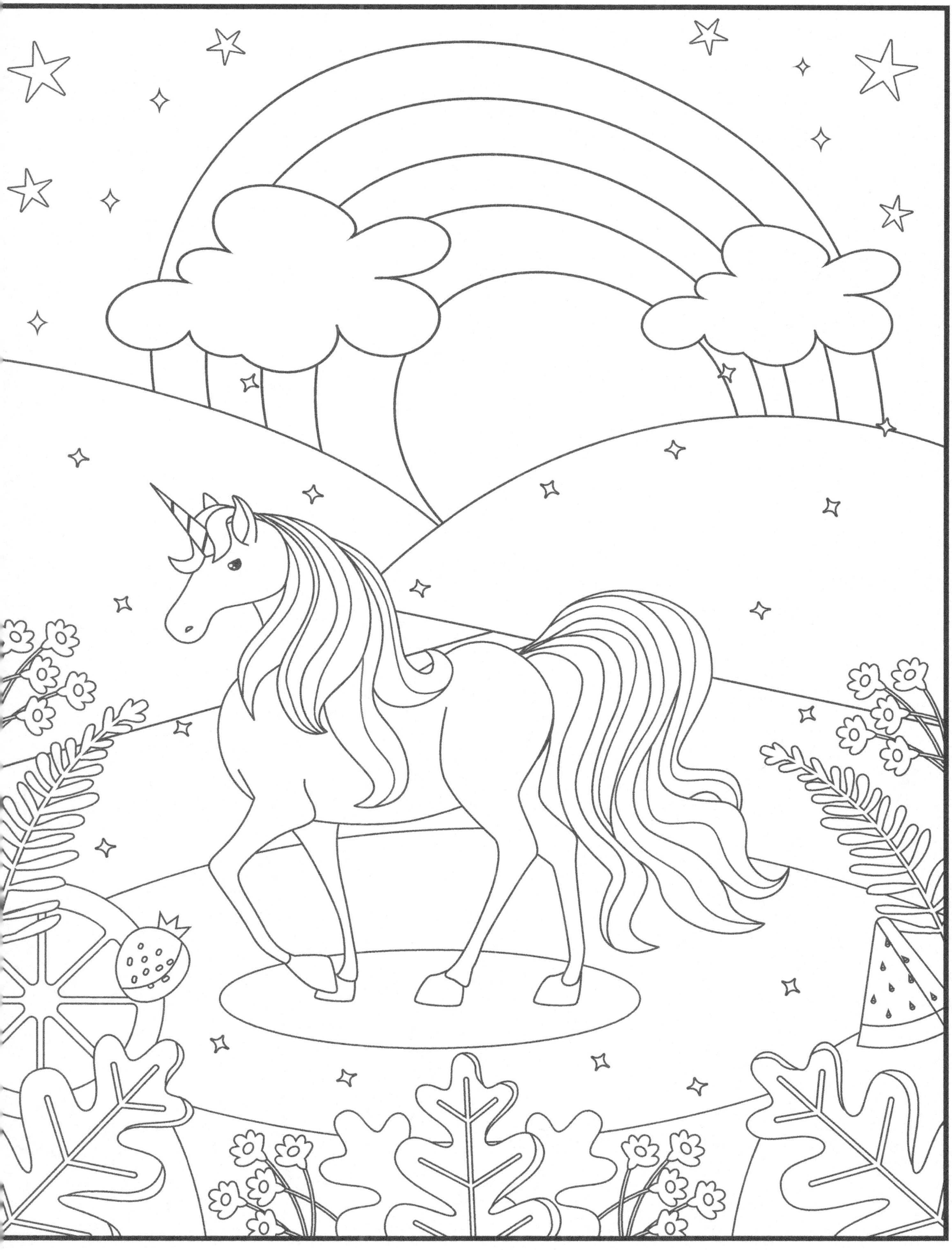

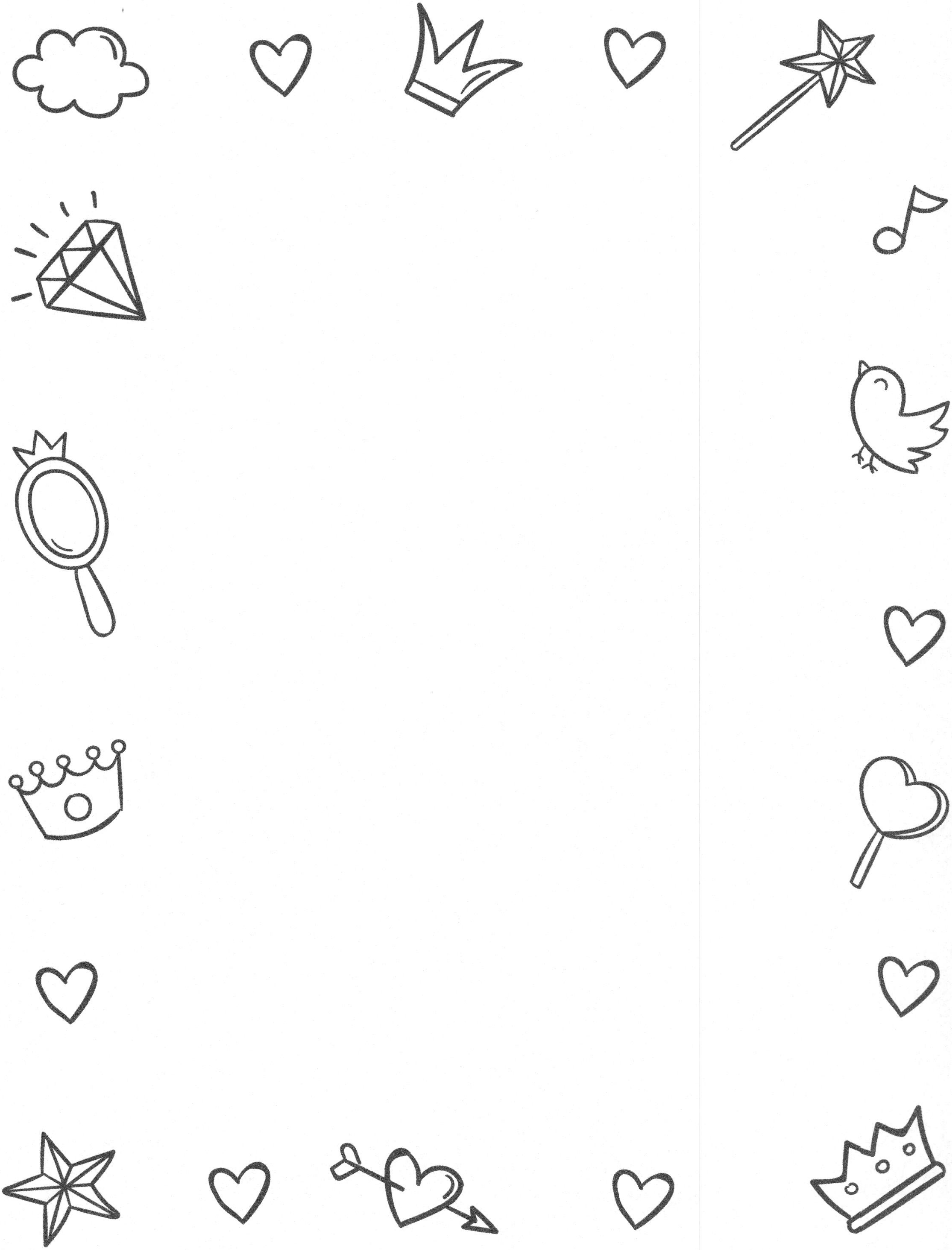

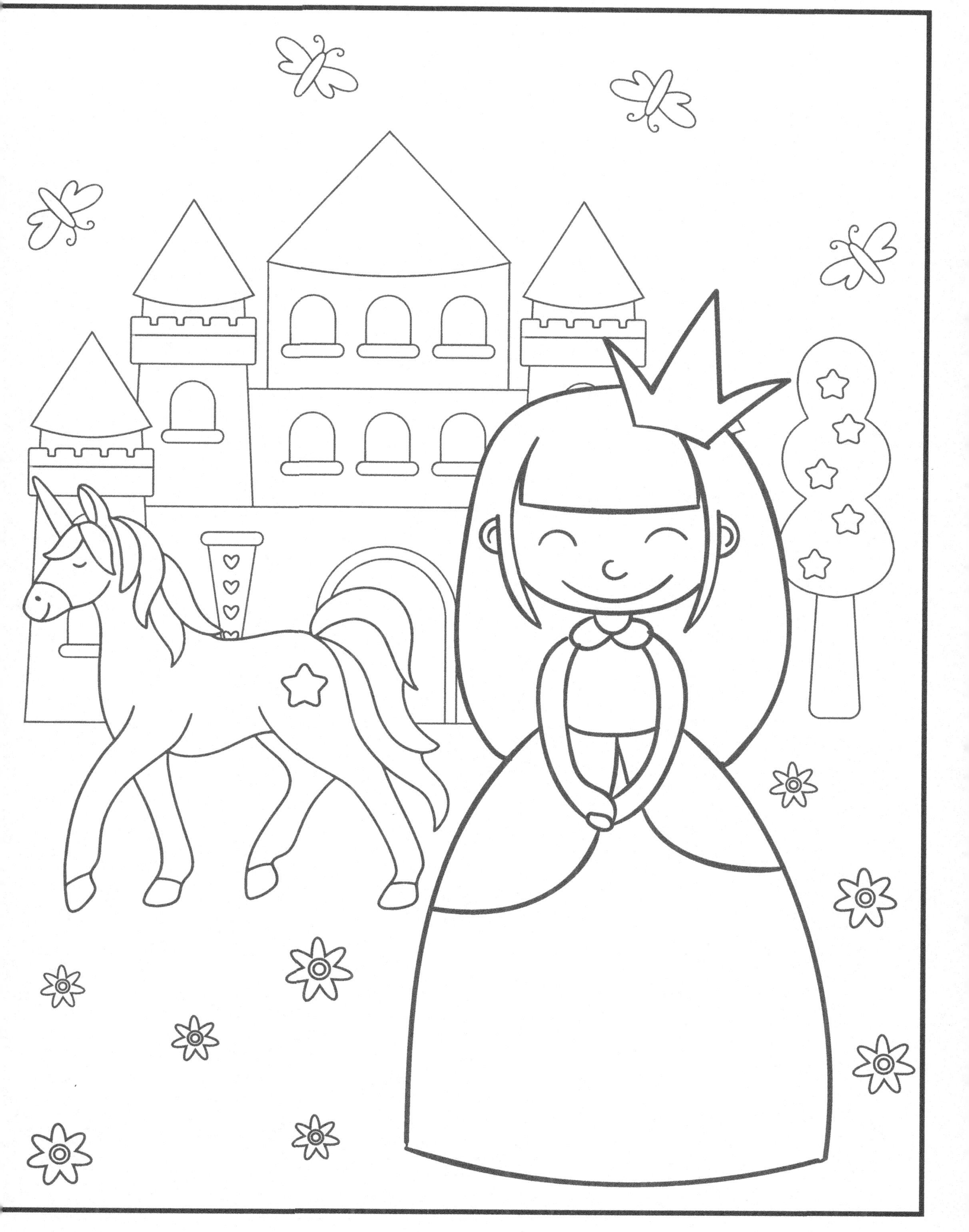

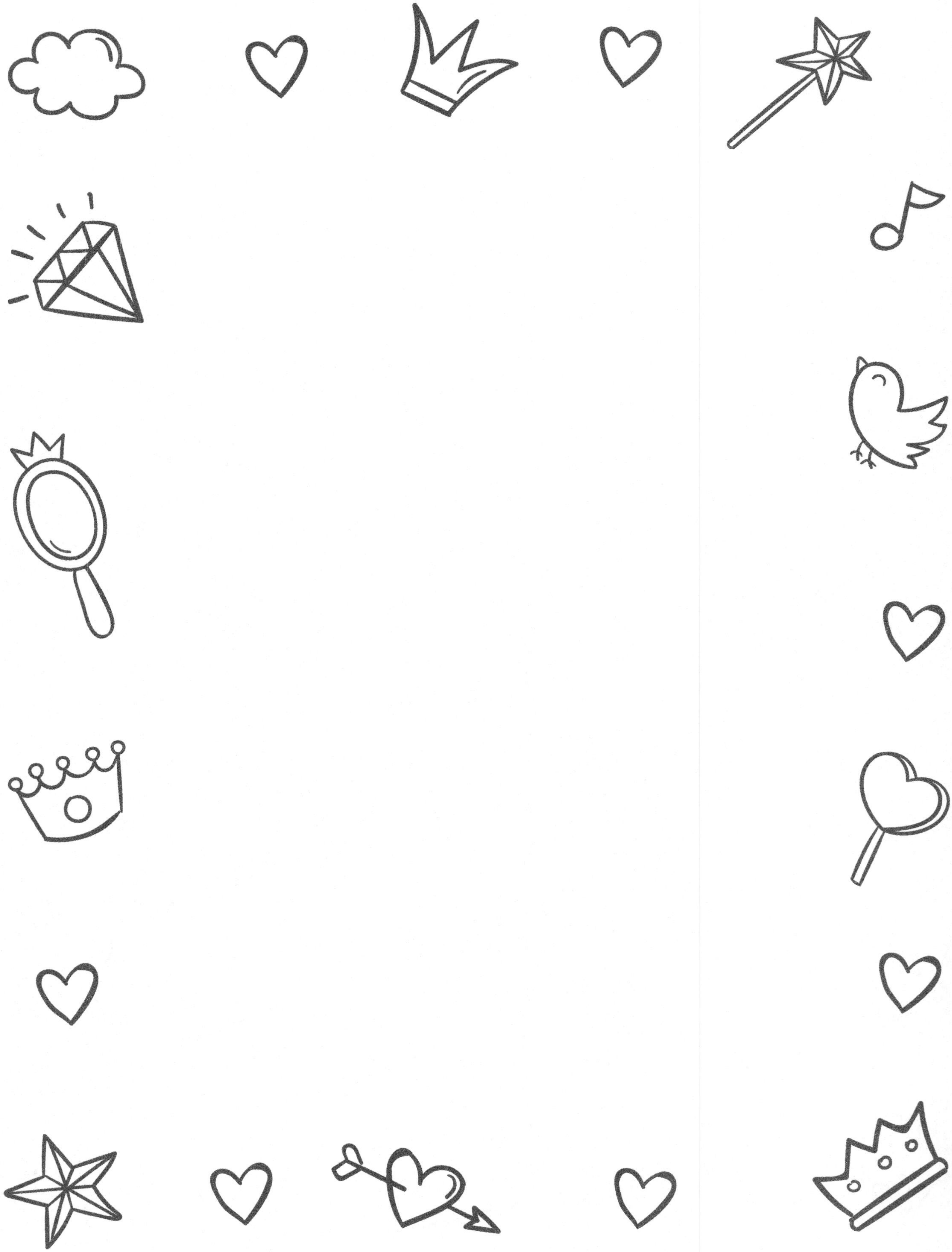

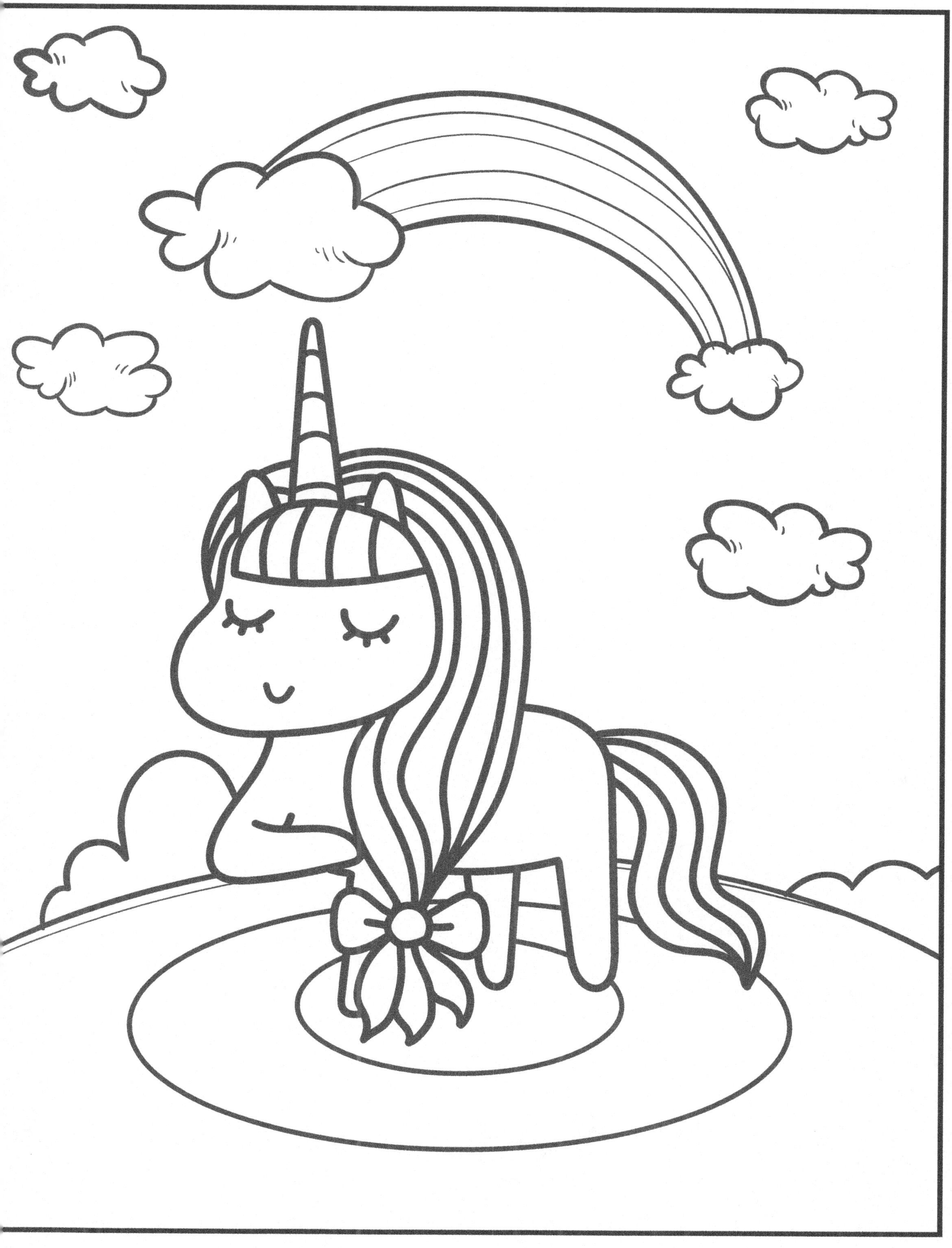

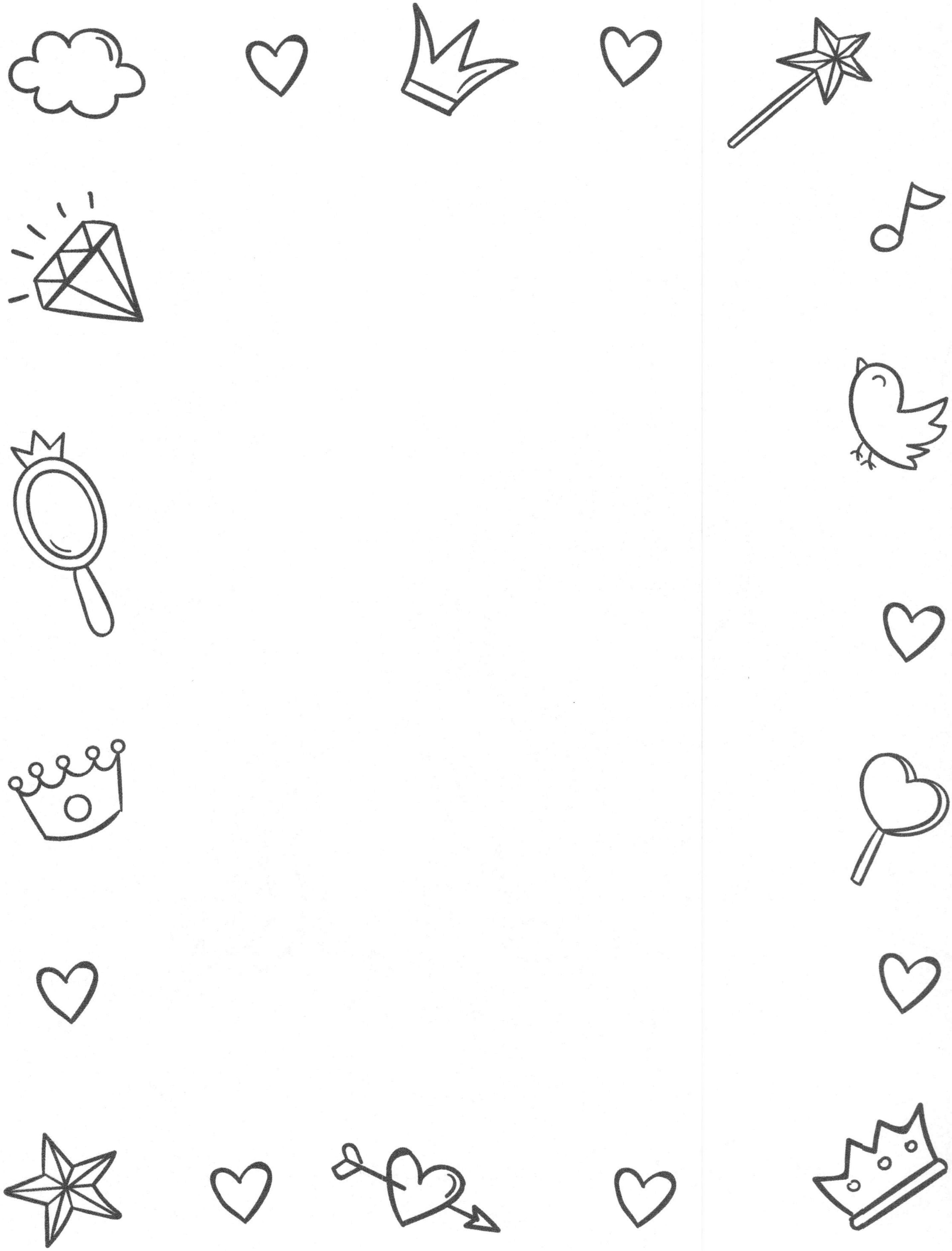

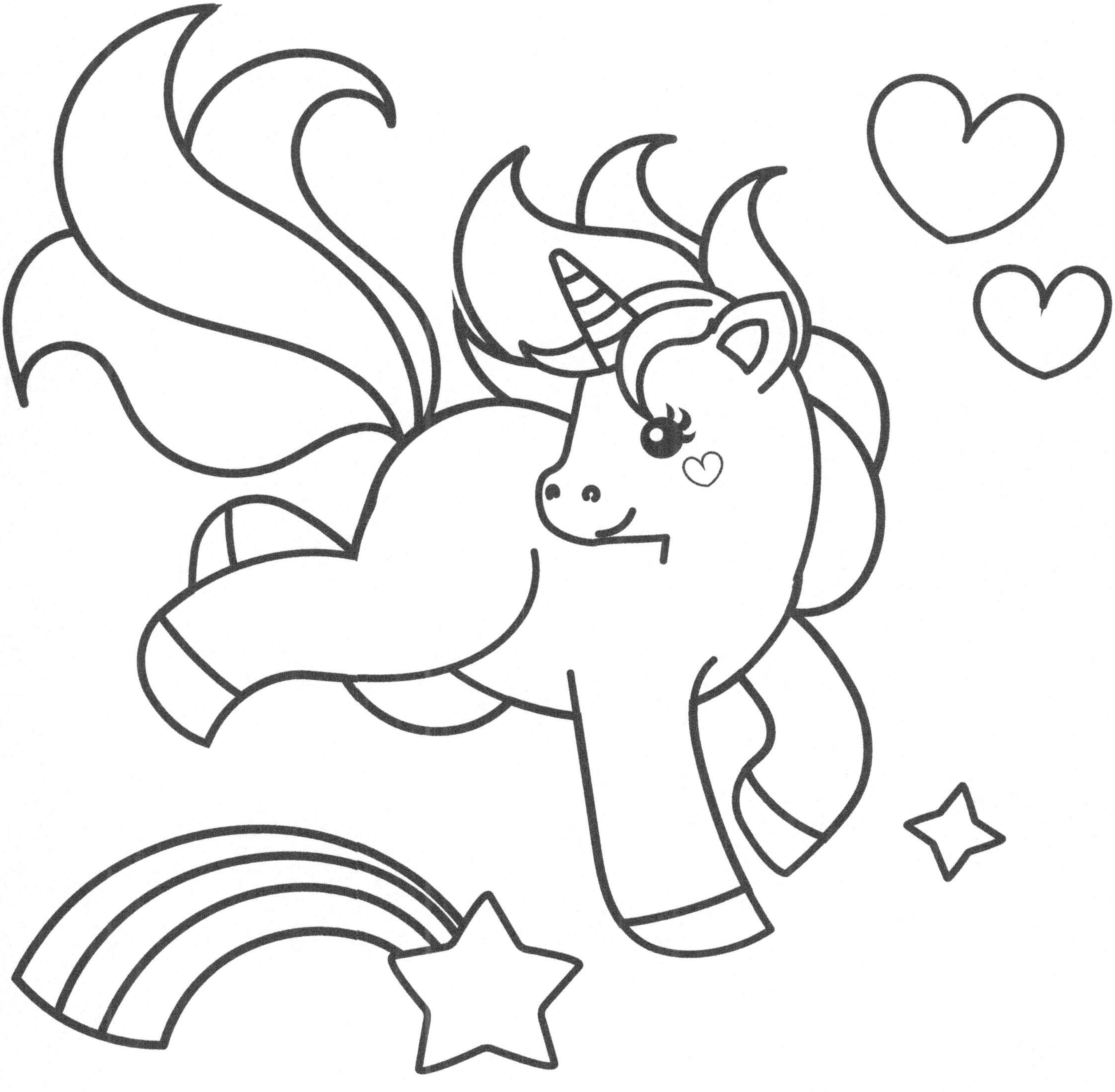

STRONG BIG SISTER!

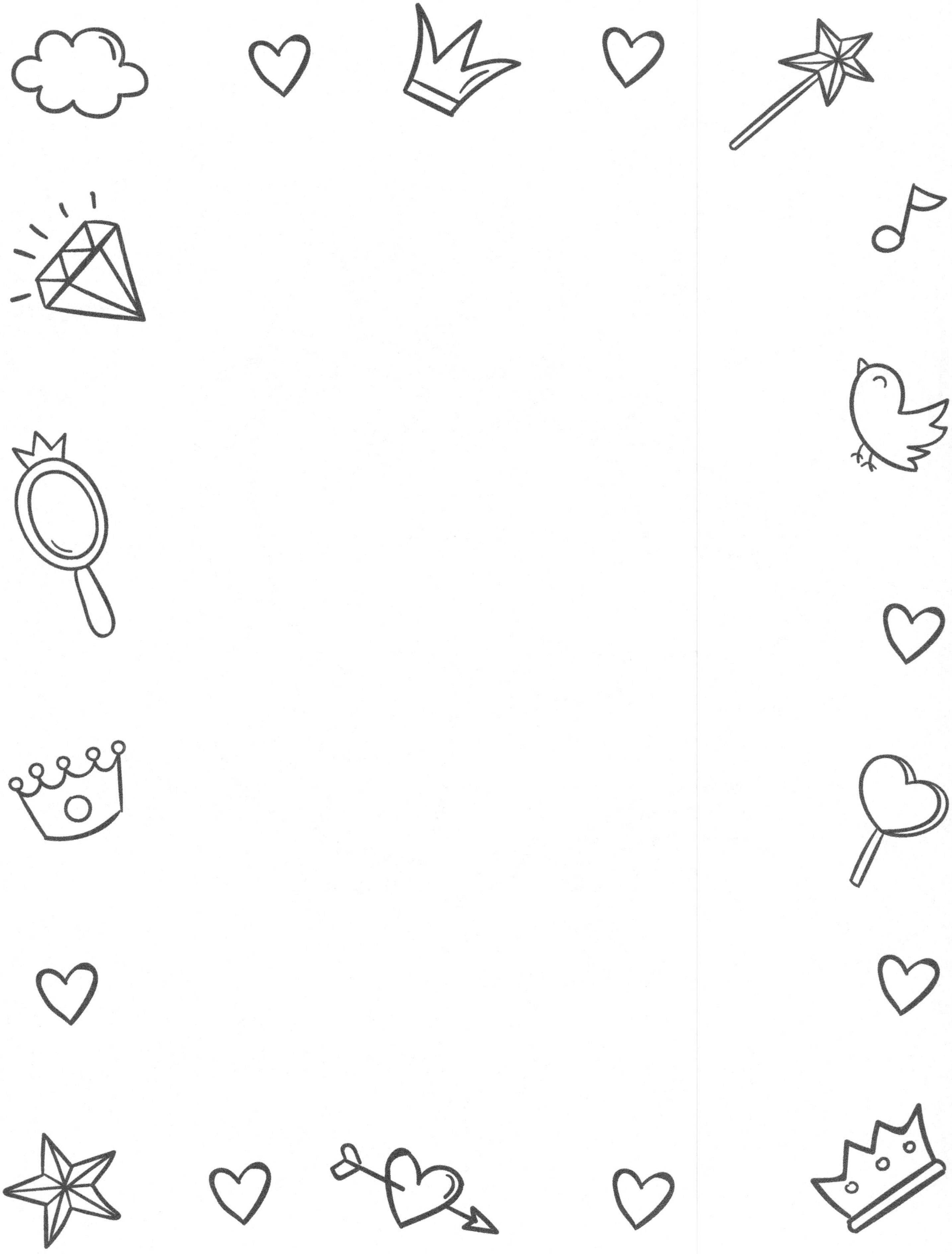

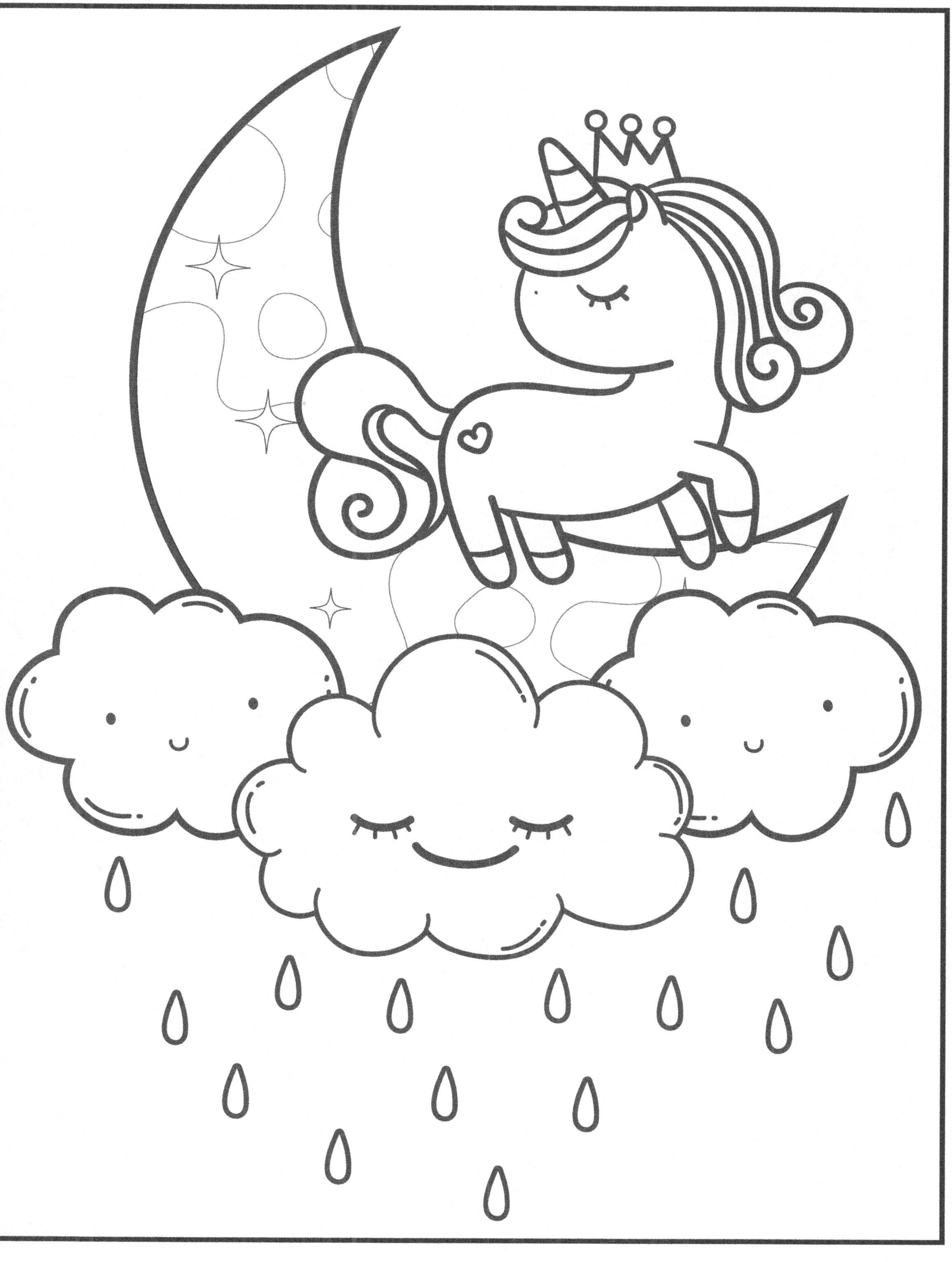

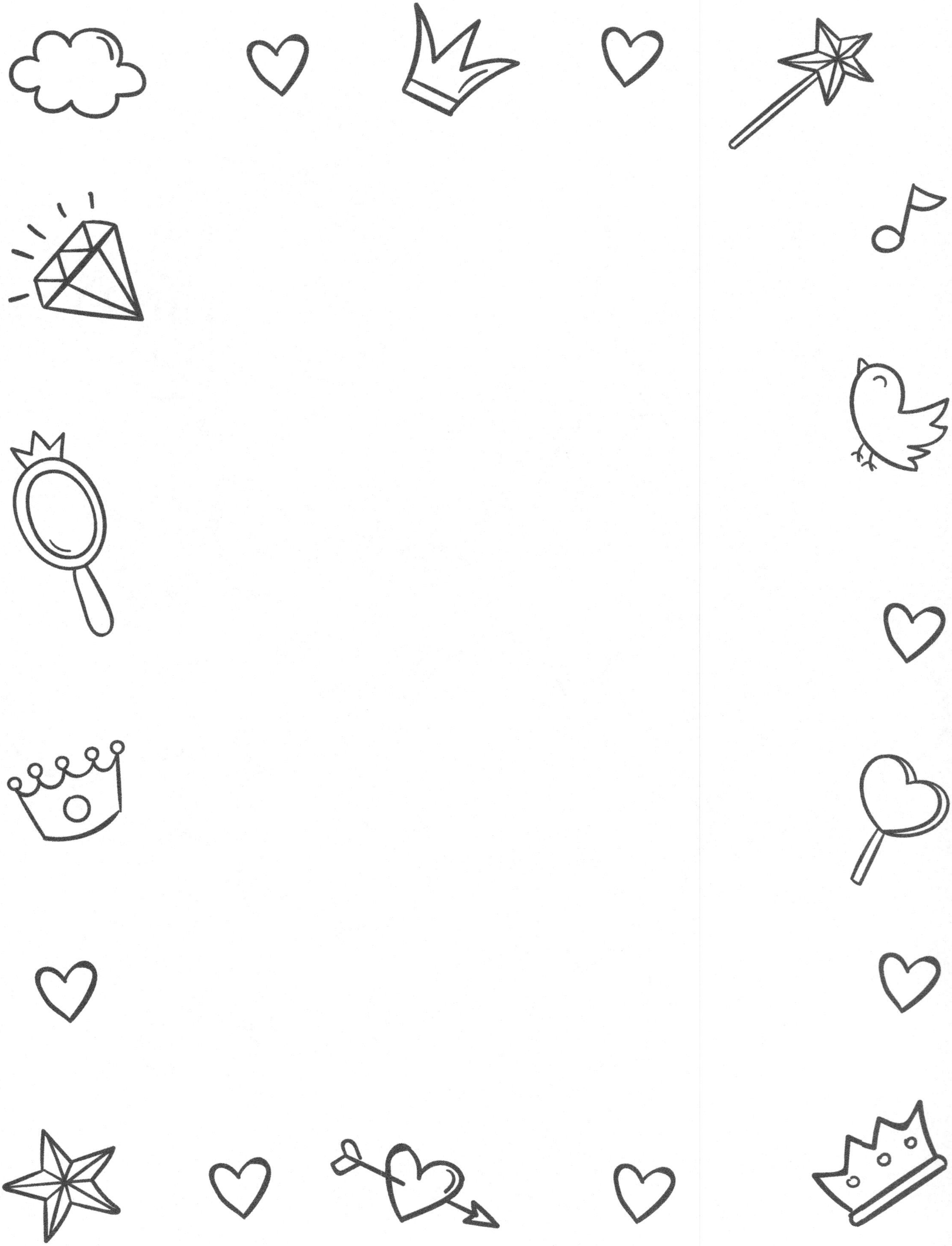

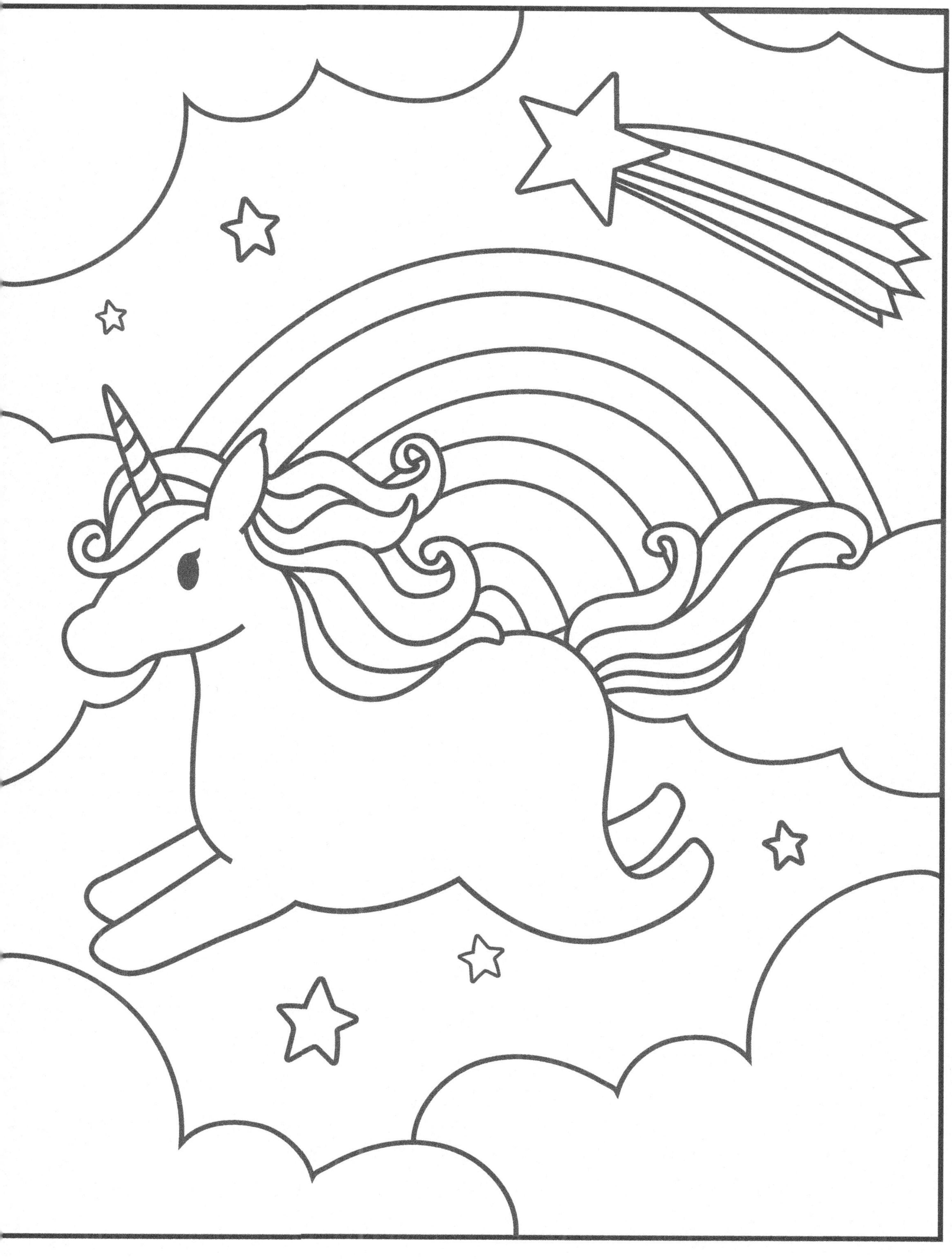

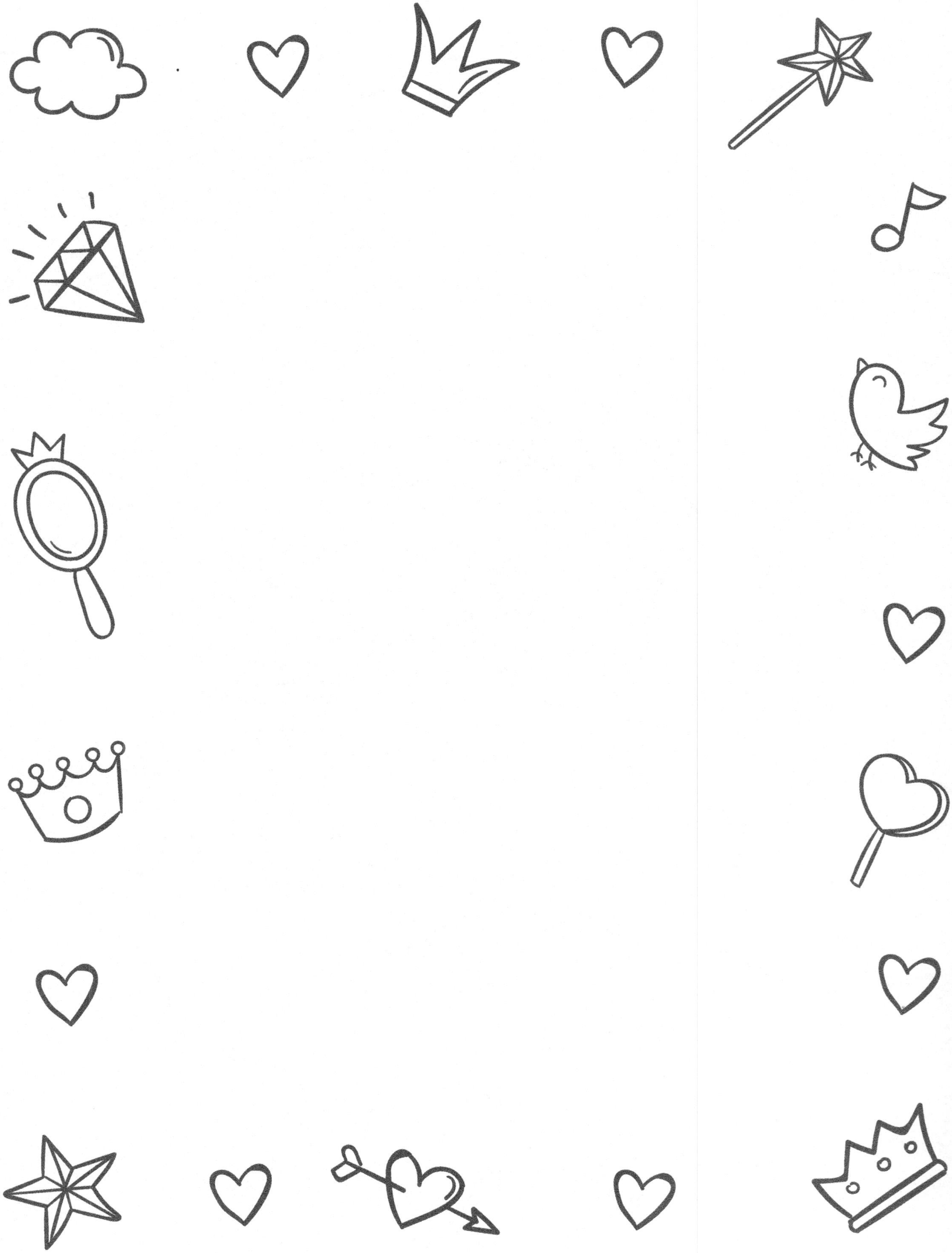

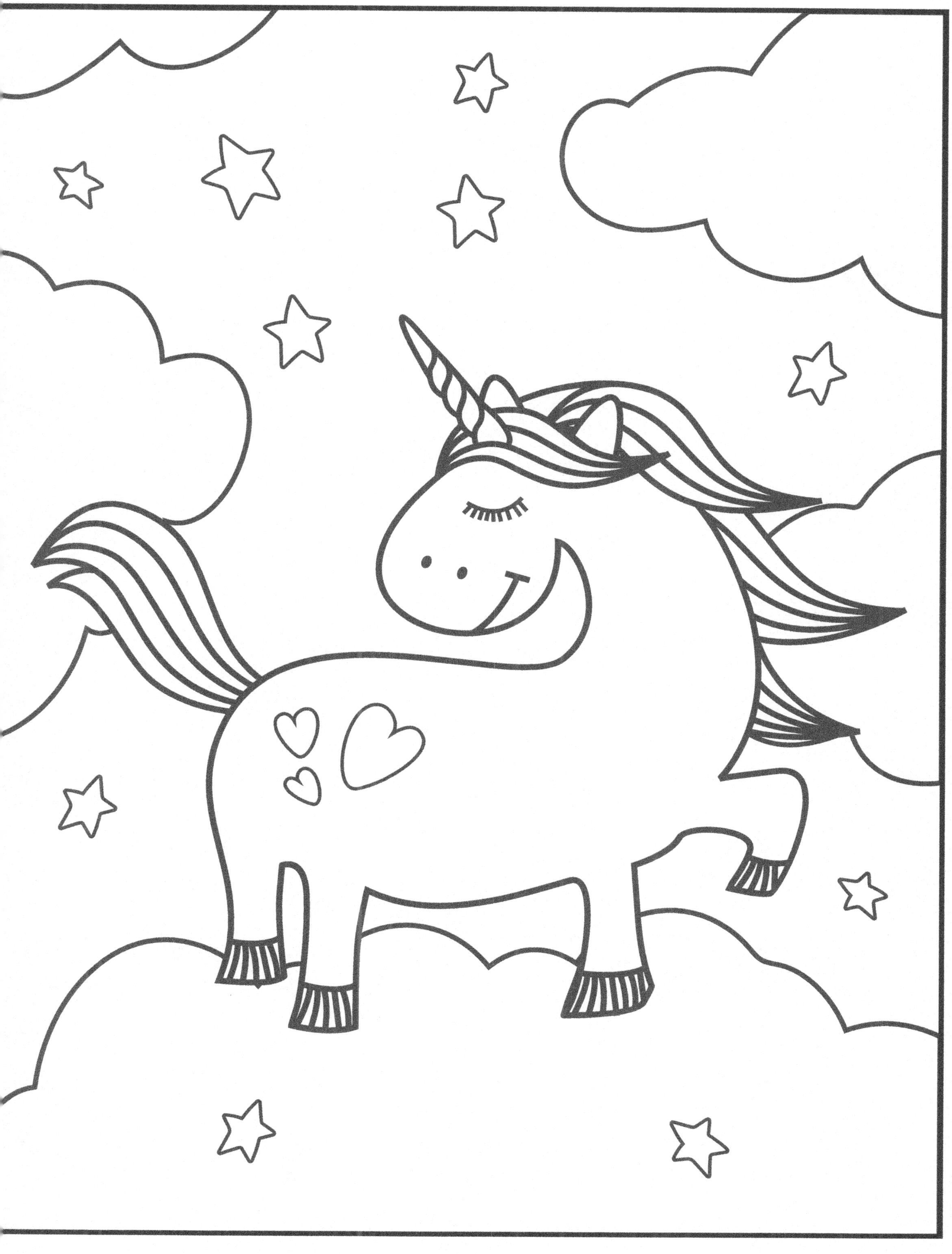

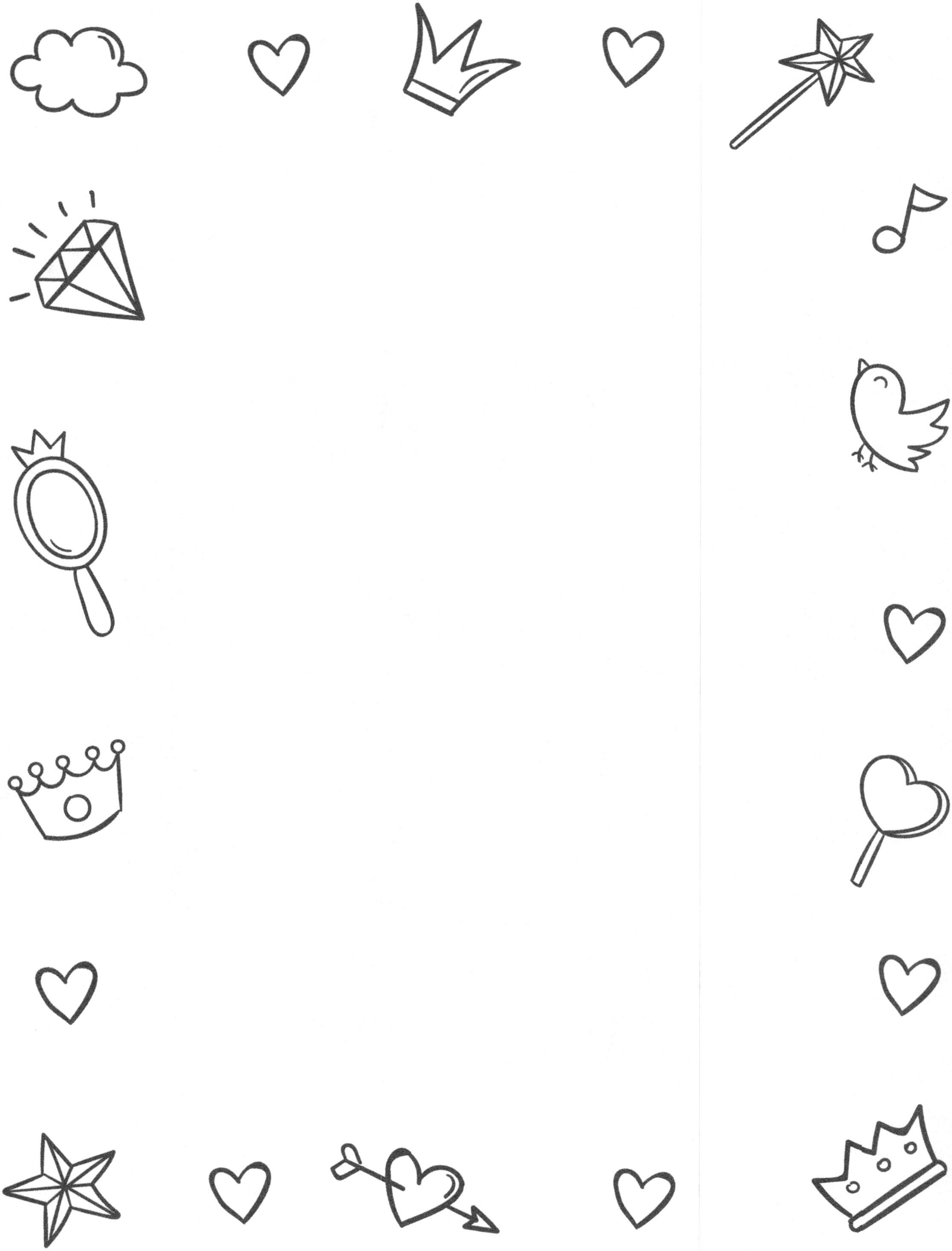

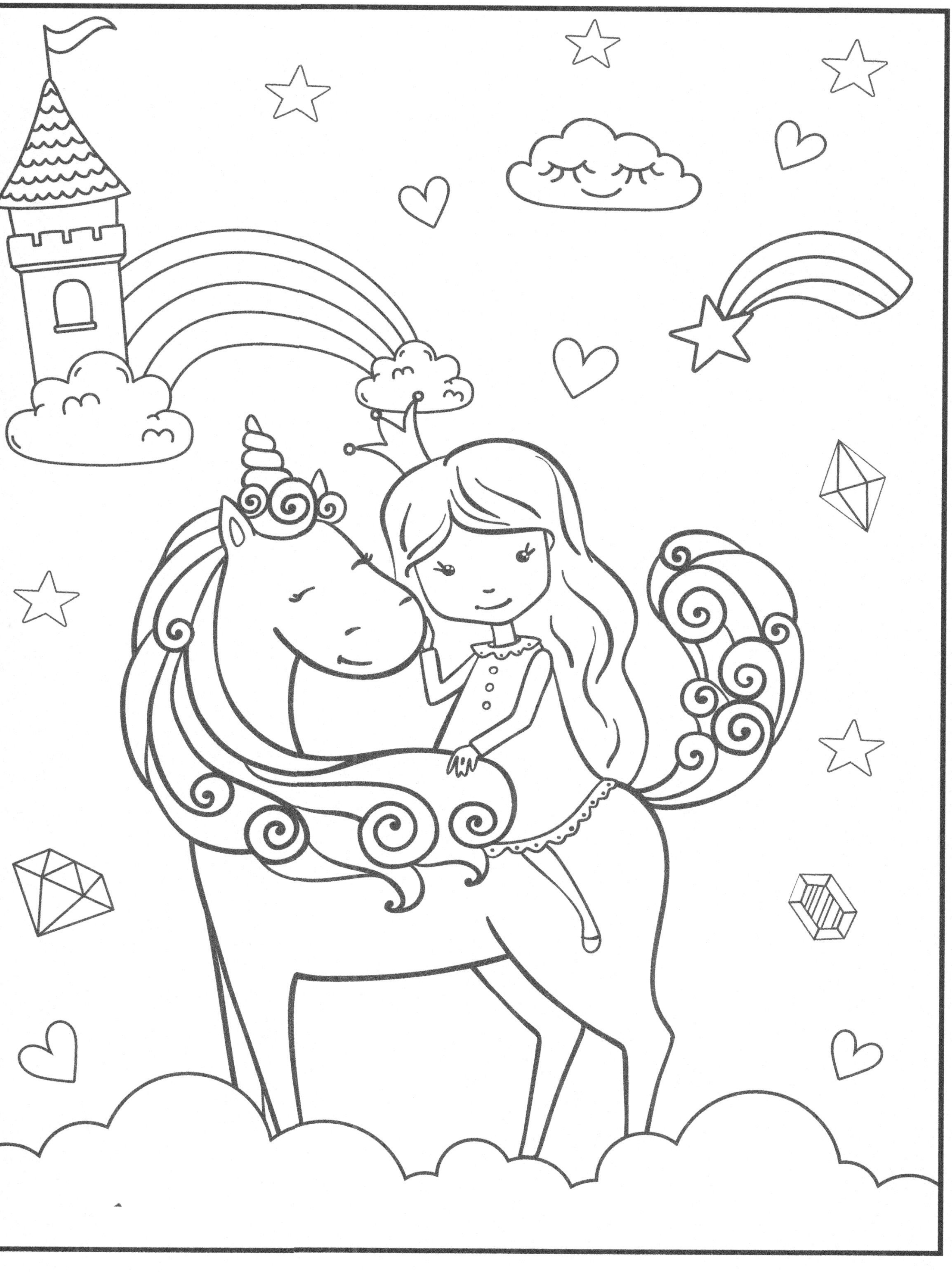

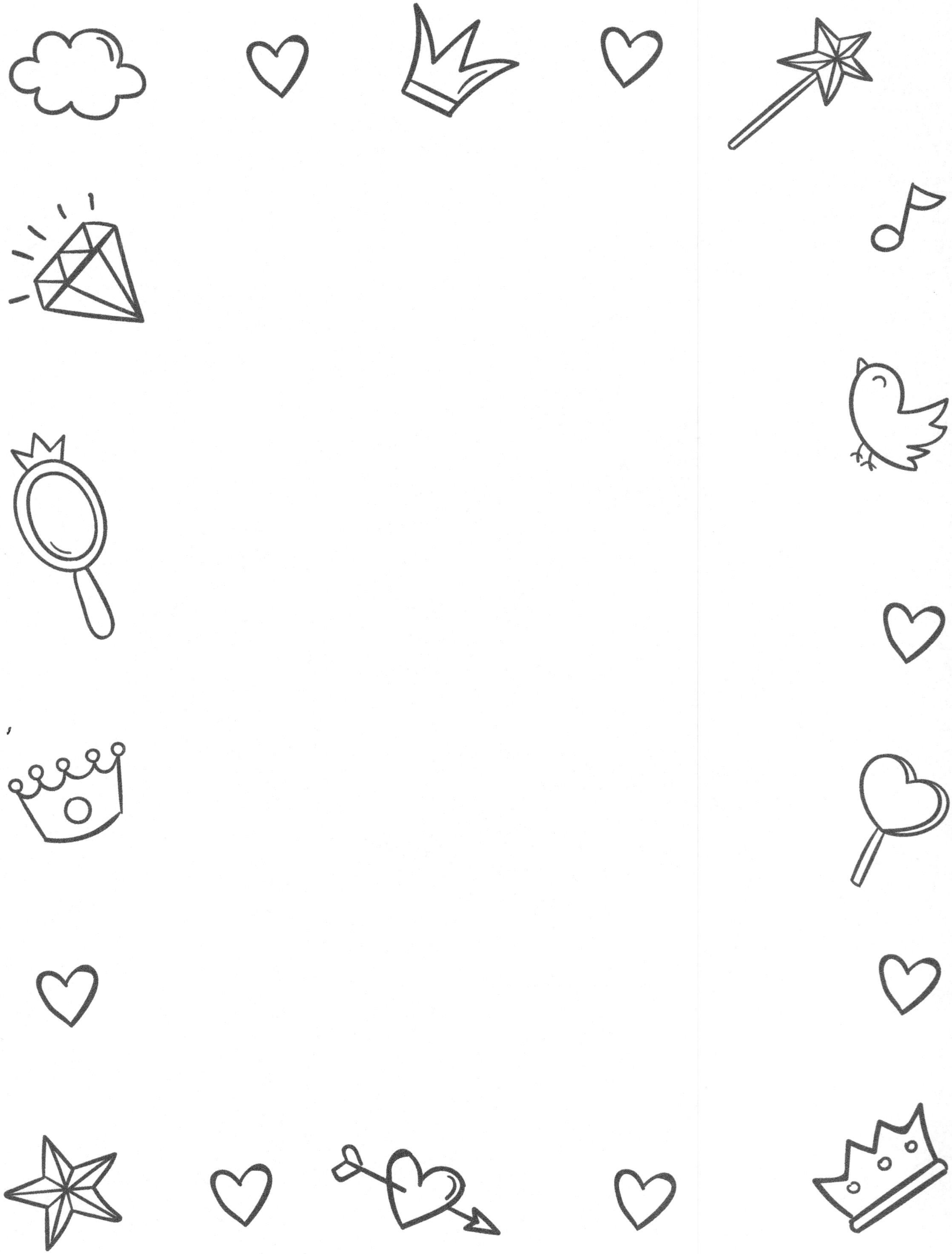

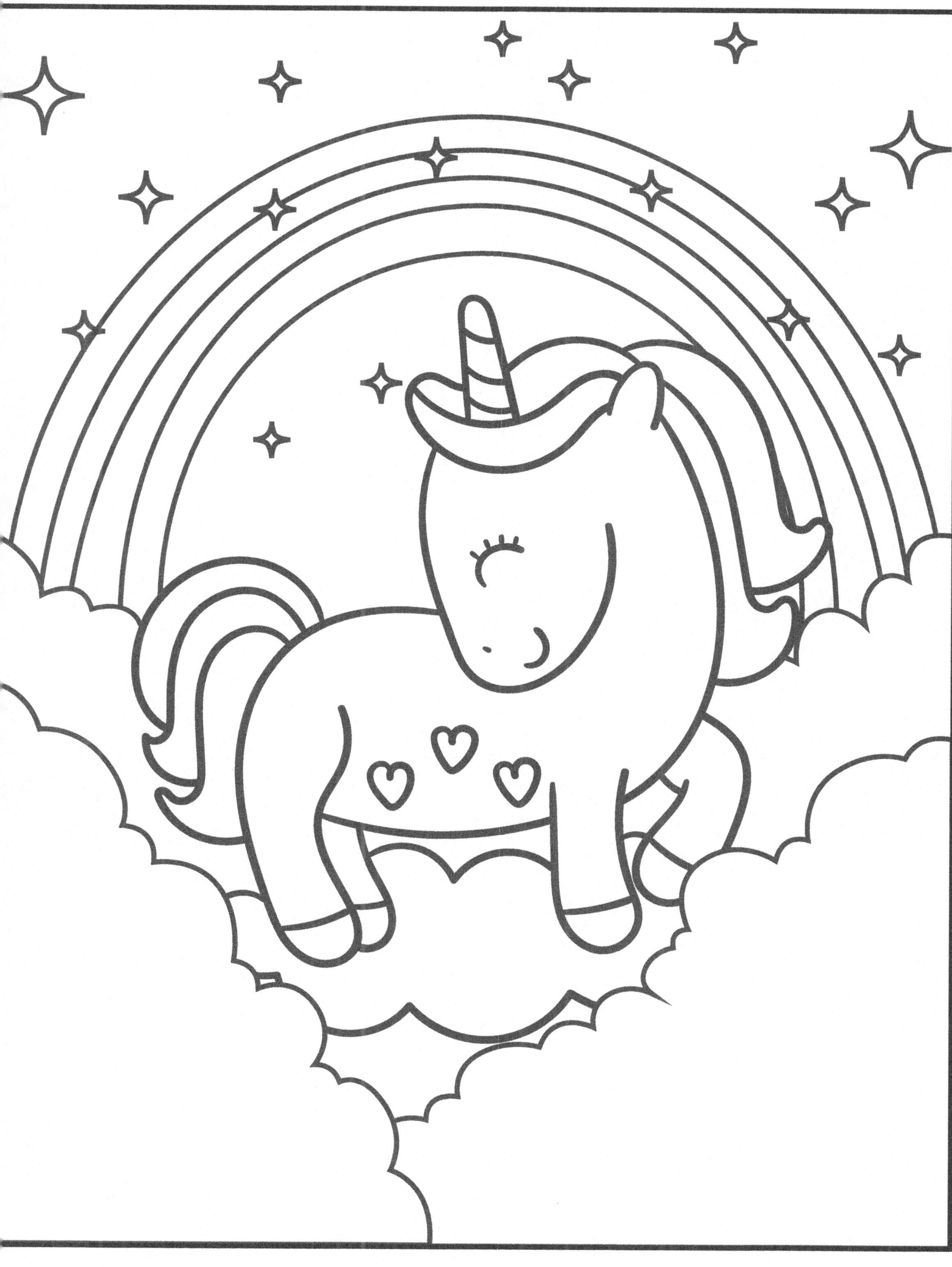

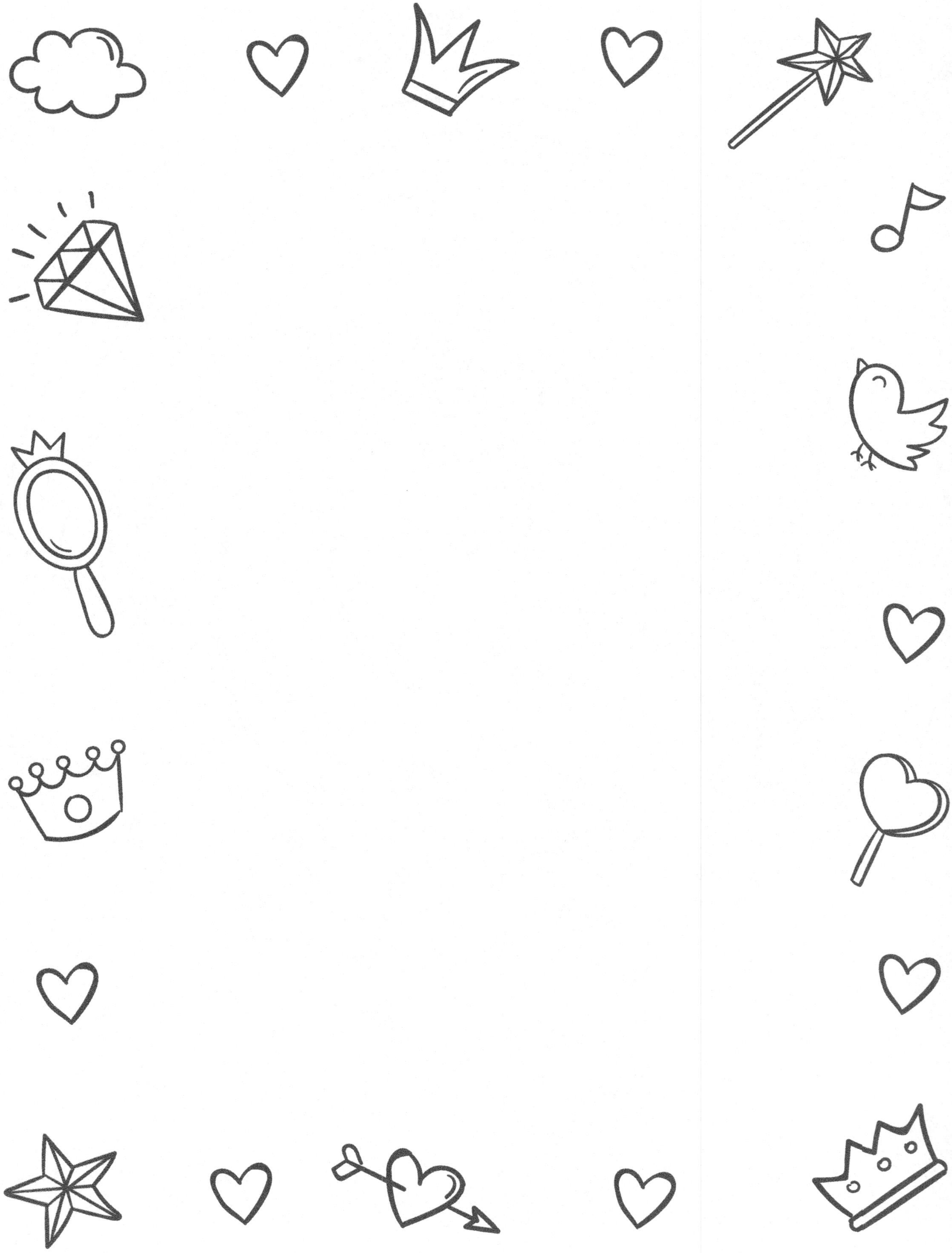

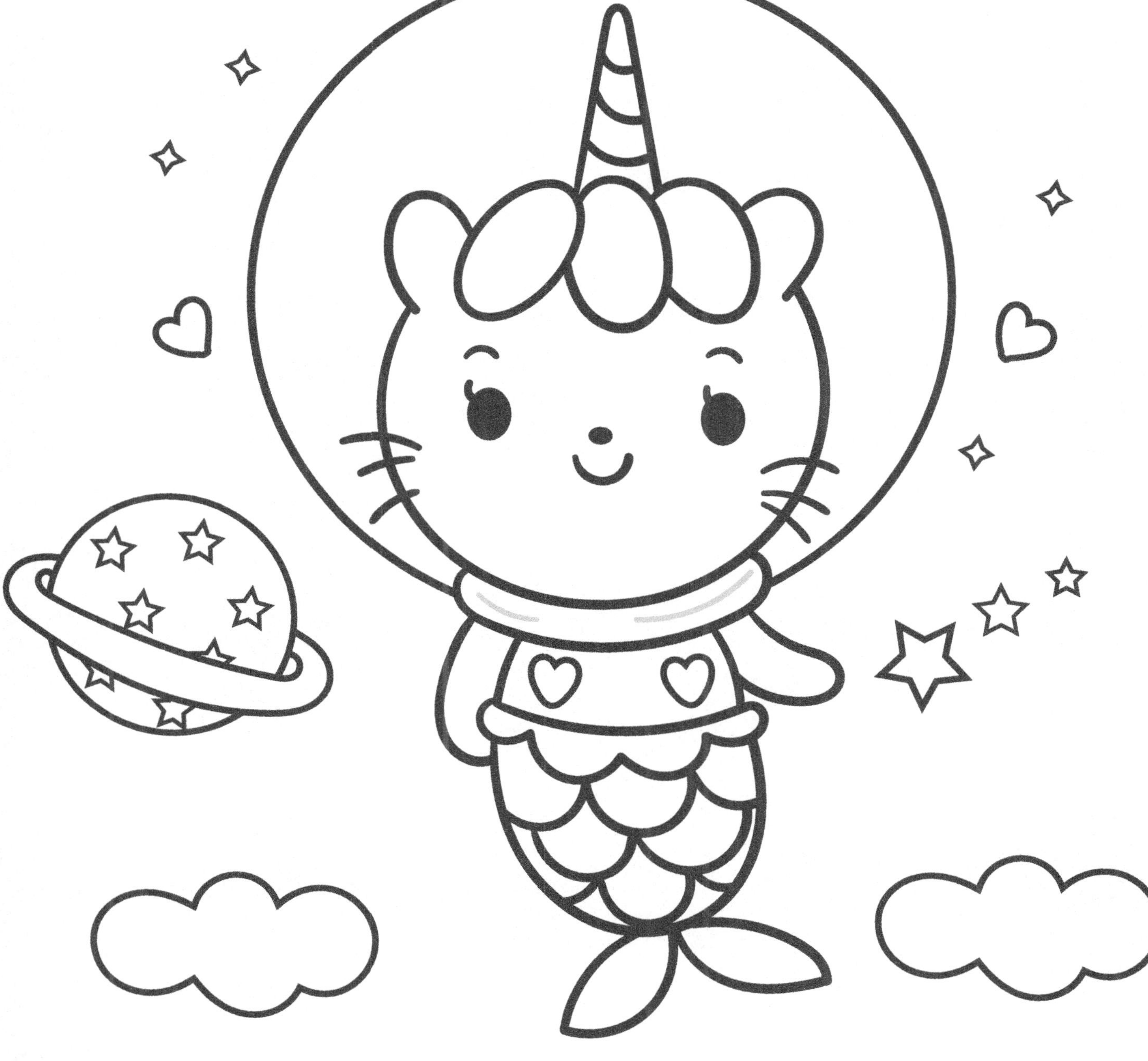

FOLLOW YOUR DREAMS

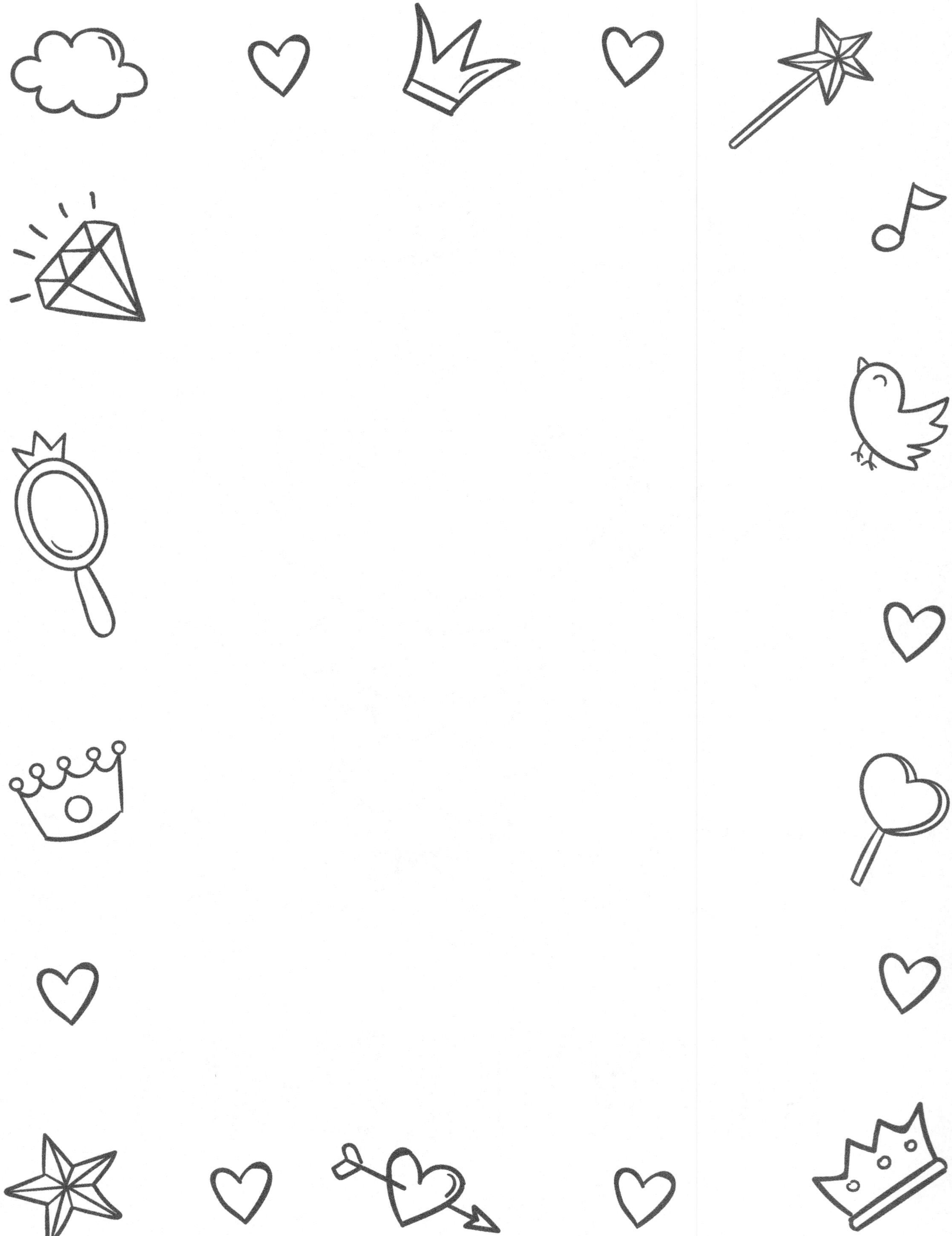

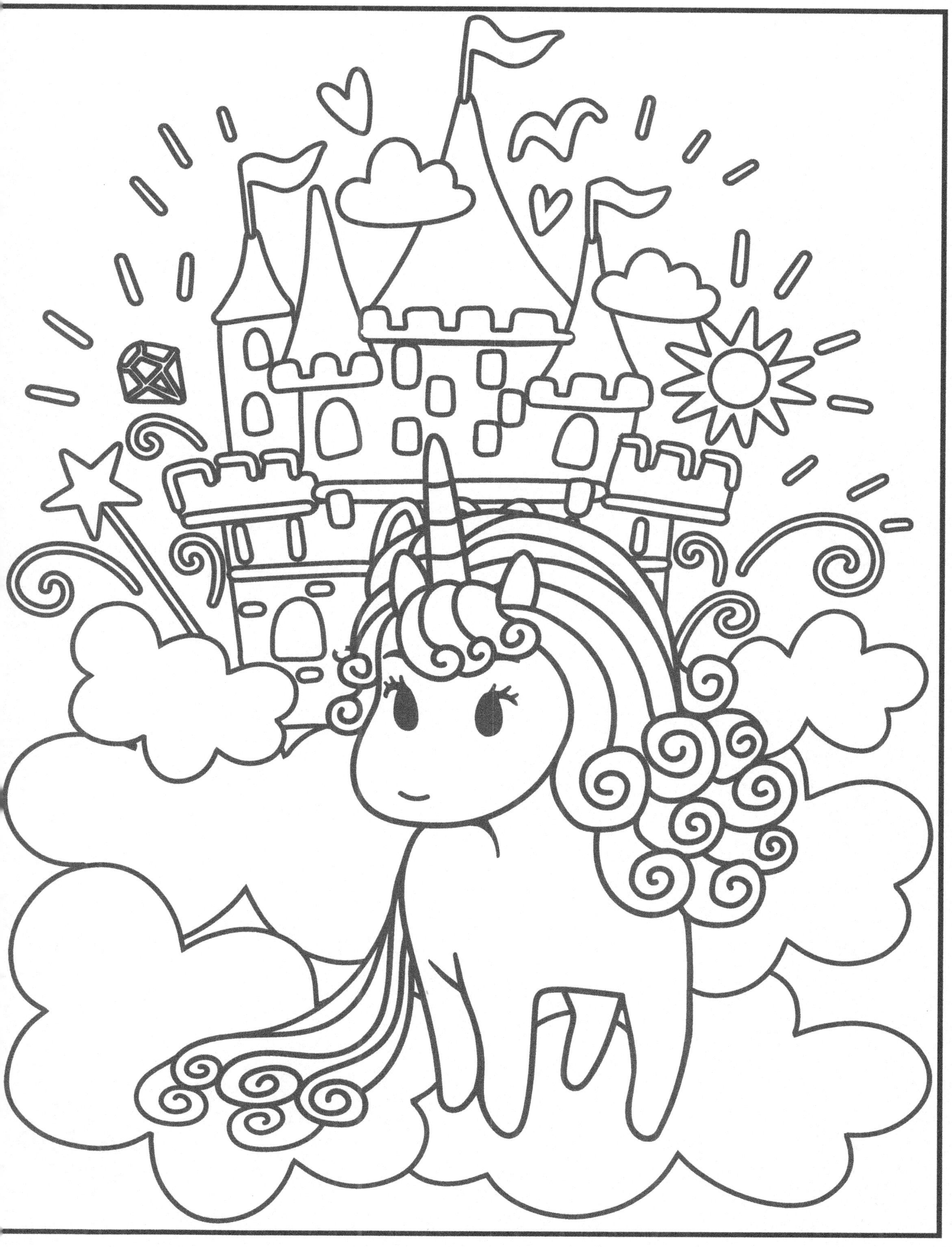

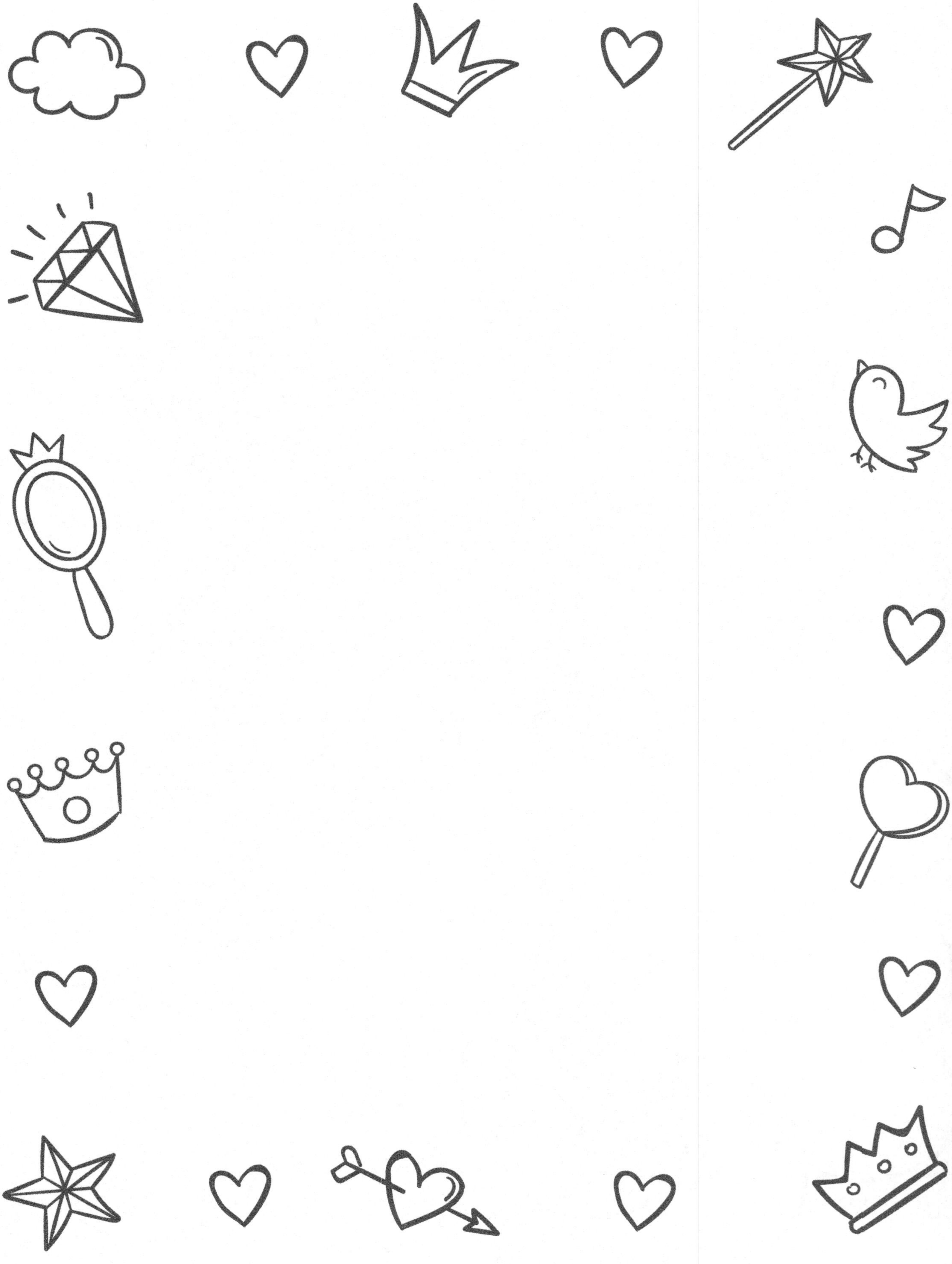

Made in the USA
Monee, IL
21 June 2022

98378535R00037